The Energetic Nature of Money

An Effective Way to Earn Wealth and Harmony In Life

By

Emil Howthorn

this book are for clarifying purposes only and are owned by the owners themselves, not affiliated with this document.

Table of Contents

Introduction

If you are willing to increase your earnings, you can. I do not care how many times you have attempted and failed or how often you have found yourself center stage at the checkout desk, acting amazement and anger: "A Refusal? That is inconceivable. Are you able to run it once more?" Regardless of how out of reach it may seem at the moment, you can earn a lot of money. Even I am-going-to-buy-everyone-I-love-a-house-and-a-gold-tooth money, if that's your thing.

I would also like to emphasize that there is nothing fundamentally wrong with you if you have not figured it out yet. Money is one of the most charged topics imaginable — we love money, obsess over money, despise money, resent money ignore money, crave money, hoard money, and badmouth money.

It reminds me how we have been socialized to deal with sex, another gold medalist in the Competition of Topics That Completely Frighten People. When it comes to generating money and having sex, you are expected to know everything about what you are doing and be an expert at it, but no one teaches you anything. You are never allowed to discuss it because it is inappropriate, nasty, and not very classy. Both money and sex can bring unimaginable joys, give birth to new life, while it can also provoke violence and separation. We are embarrassed if we do not have it, even more, embarrassed to confess we want it, and we would do anything to obtain it.

The good news is that if, like the majority of people, you have a bad or complicated relationship with money, you can heal it, transform it, and become such amazing friends with money that you wake up one day in the midst of life you have always desired. And you can begin implementing this adjustment immediately. All you have to do is to become aware of what is holding you back, make fresh, powerful choices regarding your focus, educate yourself about money, and go for it as you have never gone for it before, which is precisely what this book will assist you in doing.

The Law of Making Money

It all begins with the establishment of a particular, definite plan. To accomplish a goal, we must create a road plan that will direct us there. Without direction in our life, it is easy to find ourselves in a rut.

The subconscious is a detail-oriented creature, and the more precise you can be, the better it is. For example, in the case of finances, it would be prudent not to state, "I want to be a millionaire simply." Rather than that, specify a specific amount, a date by which you intend to accomplish your goal, and the means (or stages) by which you intend to achieve that goal. Things do improve, frequently in miraculous ways. With an open mind and a positive attitude, you will discover a purpose and a path to your desired destination. Be patient; the Universe will offer signs in a variety of ways, so remain vigilant.

Once you have identified your mission, begin by writing it out confidently in the present tense. Daily, in the mornings and nights, immediately before bed, read and repeat it incessantly. You will be programming your subconscious mind with your objective.

You must have faith in the Universe, and something will materialize. It is the epitome of the law of attraction. You will attract the object that occupies the majority of your thoughts, which in this situation is money. This is a LAW.

The trick here is to broaden your thinking and discover what you genuinely adore. Begin brainstorming about the things that offer you happiness.

Make a list of everything you intend to manifest by hand. Consider the big picture here. Determine the direction you want your life to take and set a goal for it. The act of handwriting leaves a more permanent mark on your mind. When we physically perform the actions and see our own writing, we have a much easier time believing and remembering.

When setting a goal, attention to detail of the result is critical. Indicate precisely what you wish to do, as in a specified sum of money. Additionally, put down three strategies for reaching this aim. Include a precise date for when you intend to achieve it. The idea is that having a specified real-time range motivates your thinking. Most importantly, include what you will provide in exchange; nothing is free.

Maintain some realism here; for instance, do not deposit $5 million by Tuesday and immediately go out and play the lottery. Your subconscious will dismiss this.

Proceed to write your declaration by hand on a scrap of paper or an index card. At the conclusion, sign your name, assuring yourself that you will follow through. Place this piece of paper next to your bed or on your bathroom mirror and read it every morning and evening before bed.

When you are awake, your brain contains colloquially referred to as "baby neurons," which develop during sleep cycles. Train those new cells immediately. This is a wonderful moment to acquire new skills.

This book will discuss everything you need to know about money and how it functions. You will learn about the history of money, the different types and the main factors on which money depends. Once you know about the "whats" and "whys" of money, it will be effortless to learn about "how" to make money.

Reread this just before going asleep. This is the final opportunity you will have to influence your subconscious mind before you "knock out," and while you doze off, your subconscious mind continues to work. Another excellent time to learn something new is just before bedtime.

Chapter 1: The History of Money

Anything that serves as a medium of trade is referred to as Money. Anything that can be widely accepted as a means of payment qualifies as a medium of exchange.

People were content to produce, do, and develop things for one another long before Money was invented. They may recall almost everything that transpired in isolated locations in terms of receipts and payments. Maintaining a record of and counting these transactions helps achieve the critical criteria of knowing who was invoiced and who owed Money.

However, as populations increased, the number of trades increased as well. Additionally, as individuals began producing goods for the common benefit and rulers began levying taxes, accounting became more challenging to control.

Have you ever been intrigued by the nature of Money or the reason for its existence? Money is the primary medium of exchange for exchanging anything of value or for exchanging something of worth.

Nobody possesses all that is necessary. When there were no currencies or notions of Money in existence, individuals worked out how to exchange what they had in abundance for what they desired from another. That was before the establishment of the barter system. The trick was successful by substituting wheat for rice and oranges for lemons. This is all well and good, but what if someone allergic to wheat needs medication that the other does not have? Consider the following hypothetical situation: Rachel is aware that Alice is allergic to wheat and requires medication, but she is also aware that another person is allergic to grapes, and Rachel is allergic to wheat. In this case, the exchange does not work. As a result, they must locate a third individual, Monica, who may require oranges but may also possess surplus medication.

Finding someone who could easily fit into the puzzle, as Monica did in the prior case, was never easy. This stumbling block had to be surmounted. Individuals eventually evolved to embrace a commoditized system of value exchange as a result. Everyone will require a few essentials, including milk, salt, seeds, and sheep. This mechanism was nearly impenetrable. Individuals quickly discovered how inconvenient and difficult it was to store such things.

Eventually, improved approaches were discovered, such as the utilization of metal components as financial instruments. Rare metals were more expensive than common metals. Gold and silver, which do not corrode, were ranked first and second, respectively. Then different economies began minting their currency (varying-weight metal coins bearing their official seal). While metal coins and components were easier to store and move than prior methods, they were also more prone to theft. Temples intervened to save the day, and people placed their trust in them, believing that they could never be taken away. The priests would issue a receipt to the person depositing gold, specifying the quantity of gold/silver received as a pledge to accept and refund the deposit to the receipt holder. The holder of the receipt may circulate it across the market to obtain what they seek. This was the beginning of our financial system's evolution. The public accepted the receipt because fiat currency and temples were considered centralized banks.

Former currencies were always backed by a precious metal, usually gold or silver. And this structure remained in place after governments and banks took the role of temples. This is how commodity money developed as a fundamental medium of exchange for market goods and services. During the period, all forms of Money were backed by gold or silver.

Governments eventually replaced gold and silver with "fiat currency" as legal tender. It was wholly predicated on trust in the sense that civilians were obligated to participate. Fiat money lacks intrinsic value and is a product of the state alone. Currently, all Money is in the form of fiat currency. As a result, the current worth of Money is determined by the currency and production of the governments that distribute and utilize it. Nothing was more valuable in banks than the paper currencies that functioned as the medium of currency. This was the state of financial systems at the turn of the twentieth century.

The Internet was gaining popularity in the 1990s, and financial operations were being increasingly digitalized. Banks recommended consumers to go digital since there was still some dread surrounding fiat currencies, which were perishable and subject to theft. Additionally, no paper notes were expected to be printed during this period. In banks' computer networks, Money became digital numbers. Banks would have significant difficulties today if any account holder approached their bank and requested currency notes equivalent to the balance of money in their accounts. Compared to the amount of digital currency in circulation globally, the overall amount of physical Money in circulation is negligible.

1.1 Defining Money and its Forms

Money is anything that is used as a medium of exchange. Footballs would have been Money if most goods and services began accepting them as payment.

Money serves three essential functions. By definition, it is a trade channel. Additionally, it serves as a medium of exchange and a store of value.

A Medium of Transaction

The exchange of products and services in markets is one of humanity's most fundamental practices. To reinforce these transactions, people choose something to act as a medium of exchange — they choose something to act as Money.

Since the dawn of time, food has been known as one of the most basic survival needs. As a consequence, we have come to appreciate the value of food. As with everything else of value, it became integrated into the more extensive trading network, and this was one of the first human payment processes for particular goods or services. For a long time, food has been one of the highest-paid tactics, as it often aided in basic survival. This technique is still widely used in many parts of the world today. Payment methods have evolved in step with society's development, especially in more developed cities and villages. Since there were no freezers or refrigerators back then, food items such as delicacies or any meat were discarded. This created a slew of complications.

As a consequence, this matter needed to be resolved. The alternative was a more modern method of payment that would not rust or deteriorate rapidly. It had to be traded for food or other goods and services, however.

When we consider the absence of a medium of exchange, we may appreciate its importance. When goods are exchanged solely for other goods, this is referred to as barter. Since no single item serves as a medium of exchange in a barter economy, prospective buyers must locate things that specific sellers will approve. A purchaser could find a seller willing to exchange two turkeys for a pair of shoes. Another vendor might be ready to provide you with a hairstyle in exchange for a water hose. Assume you live in a barter economy and go grocery shopping. You would need to load a truck with items that the store would consider in exchange for grocery shopping. That would be a tricky proposition. You would have no idea which items the merchant would agree to exchange before you arrived at the store. Indeed, in a barter economy, the complexity and cost of visiting a store will almost certainly be prohibitively high. Consider for a moment how difficult it is to live in a barter economy, and you can understand why human societies eventually prefer anything more than one thing—a medium of trade.

A Currency Unit of Measure

When someone in the United States is asked how much they have paid for something, they will respond with a dollar amount: "I have paid $75 for this device," or "I have paid $15 for this pizza." No one ever says, "I have paid five cups of flour for this phone." Although that assertion is logically correct in terms of the opportunity cost of the transaction, we do not report prices in that manner for two primary reasons. One is that individuals do not walk into a store holding five cups of flour hoping to purchase a phone. The other explanation is that the information acquired would be rendered useless. Others do not comprehend what we mean because they do not see value through flour as a currency. Rather than that, we quantify the worth of things in monetary terms.

Money serves the purpose of a unit of value, a structured system for determining the worth of items. We use Money in this way because it is also a medium of exchange. When we express a product's or service's price in monetary units, we represent the price that another individual would pay to obtain the product or service.

A Store of Value

Money's third characteristic is that it acts as a store of value or an asset that holds its value over time. An example would be when I found a $100 bill in the pocket of my jeans I wore a few years back. I was overjoyed. The reason for my joy was the fact that the bill was still valuable. That small piece of paper had, in fact, "stored" value.

Naturally, Money is not the only thing capable of storing value. The storage of capital and wealth is accomplished using properties, office towers, real estate, artworks, and various other items. Money is distinguished from other forms of value storage by the ease with which it can be traded for other things. Its usefulness as a store of value stems from its use as a medium of exchange.

Money, as a store of value, may serve as a basis for future payments. When you make loans, you typically enter into a deal agreeing to repay the debt in instalments. Since Money serves as a store of value, these transfers will be made with Money.

On the other hand, Money is not a risk-free medium of exchange. Inflation reduces the purchasing power of Money. Individuals can choose not to rely on Money as a store of value during periods of rapid inflation, opting instead for assets such as property or gold.

The following are some of the characteristics of Money:

Acceptability as a Whole:

Money is widely acknowledged as a means of exchange. As a result, it has gained widespread acceptance. Nobody denies the ability of Money to be used as a medium of exchange. Individuals can accept it as a form of payment.

Value Calculation:

The value of any good or service can be easily quantified in terms of Money. It is generally accepted as a value metric.

The Principal Agent:

Money is the active agent of an economic system. Money is needed for any commercial transaction in the modern economy. Money is required to initiate the production process.

Assets in liquidation:

Money is a highly liquid asset. It is straightforward to convert into goods and services. Among other liquid assets, debt, stock, and bills are all liquid, but Money has the highest liquidity of any liquid asset. Other liquid assets must first be converted to Money before being exchanged for desired goods or services, while Money may be traded directly.

Money Is a Tool:

The term "Money" refers to the process of purchasing desired products. Money cannot, by itself, make you happy. It is used indirectly to obtain specific goods or services that satisfy human desires.

Acceptability of Self-Selection:

Individuals freely accept Money. There is no need to obtain legal authorization. Individuals have an insatiable desire to hold Money.

Money takes on so many diverse aspects that it is difficult to discern what is and is not Money. Economists have classified Money in a variety of ways.

1.2 Forms of Money

Here are some of the most common forms of Money:

Actual Money and Account Money:

Actual Money is the Money that circulates within an economic system. It is used as a medium of trade for goods and services within a country. For instance, real Money in various countries consists of paper bills of different denominations and coins circulated. Account money is the currency category that is used to manage a country's accounts and perform transactions.

The dollar, for example, is the official currency of the United States. In general, a country's account money and real Money are identical. They may, however, vary.

Money as a Representative and Money as a Commodity:

Money is classified into two types: Representative Money and Commodity Money.

Commodity money is made of a particular metal and bears the same face value as the metal. Additionally, it is referred to as "complete capital." Representative Money, on the other hand, is typically made of inexpensive materials or banknotes. Representative currency has a lower intrinsic value than it does at face value.

Near-Money:

Money is described as entirely liquid. Liquidity is defined as the ability to instantly and continuously exchange total value for Money. The word "Near-Money" refers to assets that can be held with a minimal loss of liquidity. Deposits in Savings Accounts, Housing Societies, and other similar accounts, for example, are not Money because they are not generally accepted for debt reduction. They can, however, be quickly and easily exchanged for Money with only minimal to no losses.

Paper Money and Metallic Money:

This division is based on the nature of a unit of currency. Metallic Money is composed of precious metals like gold and silver. On the other side, paper money refers to Money made of paper, such as currency notes.

Metallic Money is a term that refers to coins that are used for only small exchanges. The government is the most popular coin issuer.

Paper money is a term that refers to paper bills used for more significant transactions. The legend reads, "I promise to pay the holder the amount of 50/100 dollars," based on the denomination of the currency note.

Simply stated, the legend indicates that the bill or coin may be substituted for those of comparable value.

Metallic Money is classified into two categories:

- Standard Money
- Token Money

Standard Money has the same intrinsic value as its face value. It is made of precious metals and is not subject to coinage limitations. Token Money is the Money with a face value greater than its intrinsic value. The penny coin in the United States is an example of Token Money. Government notes and banknotes are both examples of freely circulated paper currency.

The following are the components of paper money:

- Representative Money that is ultimately redeemable in precious metals and fully endorsed.

- Convertible paper money that the holder can exchange for regular coins. Precious metals do not entirely back it.

- Paper money is incapable of being converted into full-fledged currency.

- The government of a country issues fiat Money in times of emergency. Which is not always backed up by any contingency.

- Credit Money is another term for bank money. This is a set of people's bank deposits that are repayable upon request. Examples include checks, draught picks, money orders, and other forms of credit money.

Currency

The currency is a unit of account issued by the government or central bank of a nation, and its value serves as the basis for trading. The word "currency" refers to both circulating metal and paper money.

Bank Money or Deposit Money

It refers to the funds that individuals deposit in a bank to write checks. Customers deposit banknotes in the bank for safekeeping, financial transactions, and earning interest on their Money.

This Money is credited to the bank customer's account, which they can access at any time by cheques. Cheques are widely accepted these days as a simple method of money transfer.

Legal Tender Money

The currency that the government has granted legal tender status is referred to as legal tender money. This means that the person must accept it as payment for goods and services, and it cannot be refused in any way.

Both currency notes and coins are considered legal tender. They have the backing of the government. They serve as Money when the state issues a fiat (order). However, a person can legally refuse to accept payment by cheque because the bank cannot guarantee that a cheque will be honored if the account does not have sufficient funds.

Currency is the most widely used type of legal tender. When presented as payment, it cancels the debt. Personal checks, debit cards, credit cards, and other non-cash payment methods are rarely considered legal tender as a result.

Fiat: Currency

Fiat Currency is the Money whose worth is determined by legal means. Fiat Currency or Fiat Money refers to the types of Money or currency whose usefulness is determined by a government's requirement that they are accepted as a means of payment, rather than by their intrinsic value or promise of transformation into metal or another currency.

In this context, it is possible to distinguish between currency and Money. The term "currency" applies exclusively to state-issued legal tender coins and paper bills. However, the term "cash" refers to both current currency and credit capital. In other words, all Money is currency, but not all currency is Money.

Electronic Money

Electronic Money (a.k.a. electronic cash, digital currency, e-money, digital cash, electronic currency, or digital Money) is a form of electronic Money that makes financial transactions possible through computer networks. Electronic Money includes things like EFT (Electronic Funds Transfer) and direct deposit. Financial institutions transfer funds between accounts through computers and contact links. When economic transactions occur, a country-wide computer network can keep track of all people, businesses, and the government's debits and credits.

It conducts regular transactions without the use of paper currency. This eliminates the need for checks and significantly reduces the amount of money required.

Commercial Bank Money

Commercial bank money applies to charges against banks that can be used to purchase products and services. It refers to the proportion of a currency's value comprised of debt issued by financial institutions. Commercial banks raise capital through a process called fractional reserve banking. Commercial banks use fractional reserve banking to make lucrative loans over the value of the currency they hold. Commercial bank money is financial institutions' debt that can be exchanged for "real" Money or used to buy goods and services.

1.3 Barter Trading

Bartering is a term used to refer to a straightforward trade of goods, such as wool for milk. Direct trade was an economically successful system in ancient times. As societies developed, the downsides of bartering became apparent. Direct trade allowed you to acquire milk only when another cow owner required wool and vice versa.

IOUs (etymology: "I owe you") were the oldest kinds of Money. They were fashioned from stones, feathers, and animal teeth. This facilitated the exchange of products and services between members of the same community through an intermediary object that could be retrieved by the subsequent individual, much like we do today with Money.

Similar to bartering, these IOUs succumbed to their shortcomings. For little towns that required debt records, unregulated objects functioned well. They were, however, ineffectual in interacting with other cultures that dealt in a range of commodities. Thus began the creation of paper money.

Standardization of Money was necessary. It had to be embodied by something detachable, compact, and durable. As a result of this, the gold standard was created.

Individuals did not collect lumps of gold on evening strolls, and it was pliable enough to be shaped into coins and ingots. To prevent fraud, the coins will bear an endorsing image (typically of an emperor).

However, because the gold price determines the coin's market worth, coins made of other metals such as nickel, copper, and aluminum have been minted for millennia.

Governments worldwide continue to print and issue banknotes using cotton paper. Typically, the paper incorporates extra fabric strands, such as linen and fiber. As a result, the legislation will be more vital.

On the other hand, paper money originated in China in the seventh century. During the Tang Dynasty, notes replaced gold as the medium of exchange.

Money's historical context persisted long into the second century, with the introduction of credit cards. Credit cards, in their current incarnation, have a lengthy history as well. Instead of playing cards, mediaeval merchants carried sticks equipped with tallies. These tally sticks were comparable to IOUs (a phonetic acronym of the term: I Owe You) in that both parties received a receipt from two parts of the same stick.

Additionally, governments have begun to employ the stick to increase taxes. When England chose to discontinue the experiment, the remaining materials were burned, culminating in the country's worst fire.

As expected, the evolution of Money and the expansion of banks are closely related. Have you ever considered the roots of the term "bank"? Banks were established in ancient Greece and Rome, and the term "bank" originates from the Latin word "bench." Citizens could borrow Money from creditors sat on these benches in exchange for a charge. If a creditor cannot manage his finances, resulting in bankruptcy, his bench will be divided.

Individuals depositing valuables – such as gold – in tracked vaults in exchange for a receipt attesting to their possession of those things provided another source of inspiration for banks. Banks grew from what they were then into the gigantic institutions they are today, influencing the evolution of Money up to the present day.

Credit cards were first circulated in the 1950s. Like modern gift cards, the first bank card was intended for use at a single store or place. The card evolved into a form of digital money that can be used anywhere credit cards are accepted.

EMV, a common standard for magnetic stripe technology, now regulates debit and credit payment cards. The initials EMV stood for Europay, MasterCard, and Visa, the three corporations that provided the majority of the credit card infrastructure.

The mobile wallet, which was created to handle the proliferation of cellphones, serves as a substitute for credit cards. Users can pay for goods and services using mobile phones rather than actual cards.

People are disputing whether Money should be eternally linked to tangible government entities or subjectively priced gold in an age where everything is computerized, and internet money transfers are widespread.

Today, Money continues to evolve with new and fascinating technologies. These technologies are gaining popularity: mobile wallets, blockchain technology, internet payments, and cryptocurrency. As a result, the economic climate is transforming. Who knows, however? Banks and government bodies can regulate and standardize digital currencies.

1.4 The Gold Standard

It is a type of monetary system in which the state issues a fixed currency easily convertible to gold. Additionally, it is a term that refers to a publicly accessible financial system in which gold or gold deposit receipts serve as the principal medium of exchange and international trading standards. Any or all countries may fix their currency exchange rates following their different currencies' relative gold parity prices.

- It is based on the value of physical gold.

- It utilizes gold tokens and paper notes backed by or redeemable for gold as currency.

- Throughout human history, the gold standard was frequently utilized, frequently in conjunction with silver in a bimetallic scheme.

Since the 1930s, the vast majority of the world's economies have abandoned the gold standard favoring free-floating fiat currencies.

The gold standard is a financial system in which a country's value of currency value is inevitably connected to the price of gold. Countries agreed to trade paper money for a predetermined amount of gold under the gold standard. A gold-standard country fixes the price of gold and purchases and trades gold at that price. The set price establishes the value of the currency. If the U.S. establishes a gold price of $500 per ounce, the currency will be worth 1/500th of an ounce of gold.

The gold standard has degraded into a vague word throughout time. Nonetheless, the term is occasionally used to refer to any commodity-based monetary system that is not based on unbacked Fiat Money or Money that has value primarily due to government-imposed taxes on residents. However, significant distinctions exist.

While some gold standards ban everything but gold bullion and coins, or precious metals, others allow the circulation of other commodities or paper currencies. Earlier methods permitted only for converting the state's money to gold, severely restricting the capacity of banks and governments to inflate and deflate.

Gold is preferred as a medium of exchange by most advocates of commodity money due to its intrinsic qualities. Because gold is utilized for non-monetary applications such as jewelry, electronics, and dentistry, it can maintain a low level of actual demand indefinitely. In contrast to diamonds, it is entirely and evenly divided without losing value over time. It is difficult to wholly counterfeit and has a fixed supply — the world already has a certain amount of gold, and inflation is constrained by mining pace.

There are various advantages to the gold standard, one of which is price stability. This is a long-term good since it makes it more difficult for policymakers to expand the money supply and inflate inflation. Inflation is uncommon, and hyperinflation is improbable because the money supply can only rise in lockstep with the growth of gold reserves. Similarly, the gold standard would have defined international exchange rates between member countries and decreased global trade uncertainty.

It does, however, result in divergences across gold-standard-adhering states. Countries that produce gold have an advantage over those that do not, as the gold standard allows for increased holdings. According to some analysts, the gold standard typically averts economic downturns by inhibiting a government's ability to expand the money supply — a method employed by central banks to promote economic growth.

Coins were initially struck in gold circa 700 B.C., significantly increasing their utility as a monetary unit. Previously, gold had to be weighed and its purity was determined before settlement.

Gold coins were unattractive because clipping these relatively unique coins to collect gold that could be reassembled into bullion was a widespread activity for decades. In 1696, Great Britain's Popular Recoinage created a system of coin processing that eliminated clipping.

The United States Constitution granted Congress the authority to manufacture Money and control its value in 1789. Adopting a single national currency, an economic system that formerly relied on circulating foreign coins, set silver as it's standard currency. In 1792, a bimetallic ideal was established in recognition of silver's higher abundance than gold. According to Gresham's law, the publicly negotiated silver-to-gold parity ratio of 15:1 appropriately mirrored the pricing ratio at the time. As long as states or financial organizations held monopoly rights over the issue of national currencies, the gold standard proved insufficient or contradictory as a constraint on monetary policy. Throughout the twentieth century, the gold standard began to collapse. This process started in the United States in 1933 when President Franklin D. Roosevelt signed a bill outlawing individual ownership of monetary gold.

Following World War II, the Bretton Woods agreement obliged allies to adopt the U.S. dollar as a reserve currency in preference to gold. The U.S. government has pledged to maintain a sufficient supply of gold to sustain its currency. Nixon's administration halted the practice of converting U.S. dollars to gold in 1971, ushering in a fiat currency regime.

No nation officially adheres to the gold standard. The United Kingdom abandoned the gold standard in 1931, and the United States followed suit in 1933, eventually quitting the system entirely in 1973.

As the name implies, the gold standard is a monetary system in which the value of Money is determined by gold. On the other hand, a fiat economy is a financial system in which the currency's value is unrelated to any tangible object and can vary significantly concerning other financial instruments traded on the foreign exchange markets. The term "fiat" is derived from the Latin "fieri," which means "arbitrary deed or judgement." The significance of fiat currencies is partly because, as their etymology implies, they would be designated as legal tender by government mandate.

International business was conducted in the decades preceding World War I based on what became known as the worldwide gold standard. Physical gold was utilized to facilitate trade between nations in this system. Countries having trade surpluses amassed gold to use as leverage to increase their exports. On the other hand, countries running trade deficits saw their gold stockpiles decline as gold was used to pay for imports.

1.5 Fiat Currency- The Paper Money

Fiat Money is government-issued Money that is not backed by a tangible asset such as silver or gold but rather by the issuing state. The value of Fiat Money is governed by the relationship between demand and supply and the country's sustainability, rather than by the value of the underlying product, as is the case with commodity money. The majority of worldwide paper currencies and the British pound, and other major world currencies are Fiat currencies.

- State-issued Fiat money lacks any physical backing, such as gold.

- Because central banks can control the amount of Money printed using Fiat money, they exert influence on the economy.

- The majority of fiat currencies, including the United States dollar, are paper currencies.

- One risk associated with fiat money is that governments issue an excessive amount, resulting in hyperinflation.

Fiat money has value only if the government holds it or two contracting parties agree on its value. Historically, governments minted coins from valued tangible assets such as silver or gold or printed banknotes that could be traded for a predetermined amount of a useable physical product. Fiat money is not transferrable and cannot be redeemed.

Because fiat money is not backed by actual reserves such as a national silver or gold reserve, it is susceptible to inflation and eventually loses its value in hyperinflation.

When individuals lose faith in Money as a medium of currency, the currency loses value. This is in contrast to gold-backed Money, which is intrinsically valuable due to the use of gold in jewelry and ornamentation and the development of mobile devices, servers, and aircraft equipment.

The United States dollar is a Fiat and Legal currency approved for individual and state use. Legal tender refers to any currency that has been proclaimed legal by a nation. Numerous governments create a fiat currency that becomes legal tender when it becomes the default form of repayment.

Fiat money is a strong currency if it can perform the functions of a monetary unit in an economy: storing value, maintaining a quantitative account, and facilitating trade. Additionally, it has an outstanding seigniorage.

Fiat currencies were widespread in the twentieth century as governments and central banks sought to protect their economies from the worst effects of natural economic booms and busts.

Since fiat money is not a finite or fixed resource in the same way that gold is, central banks have significantly greater control over its output, allowing them to manage economic factors such as money velocity, credit supply, interest rates, and liquidity. For instance, the Federal Reserve Bank of the United States has a dual mandate to manage inflation and unemployment.

On the other hand, the 2007 housing slump and ensuing financial meltdown lowered hopes that central banks would employ monetary policy to avert depressions or severe recessions.

Due to the restricted quantity of gold, a gold-backed currency is more resilient than fiat money in general. In contrast to commodities, Unlike gold bullion or redeemable gold and silver paper currency, fiat money is guaranteed by the state that issued it. One reason is that governments desire that you pay taxes with their fiat money. Individuals will accept it if they are required to pay taxes or risk harsh fines or imprisonment. As with the credit theory, some money theories assert that because all currency is a credit-debit connection, it is irrelevant whether it is supported by anything to preserve its value.

Today, every nation uses Fiat money as legal tender. While gold and gold coins are readily available for purchase and sale, they are rarely traded or utilized in everyday transactions, making them a more speculative asset.

Over the last few decades, most Fiat currency nations have seen only brief bouts of inflation, averaging less than 2% per year on average. A low level of inflation is viewed positively as a stimulant of economic growth and expenditure. It incentivizes clients to spend their money rather than allowing them to squander it and lose control over time. Although governments theoretically can print "infinite" amounts of Fiat money units, they rarely do so in practice. Many Western central banks are tasked with maintaining a generally stable and resilient currency, yet a progressively devalued currency is detrimental to trade and access to financing.

Additionally, it is disputed if "runaway money printing" results in hyperinflation. Since Money was based on precious metals, hyperinflation has occurred throughout history. Both modern hyperinflations began with a structural decline in the country's natural growth economy and political instability.

1.6 Digital Money

Before we get more into the concept of digital money, let's consider an illustration. John's day is filled with many errands. Listed below are a few of these:

- Utility bill payment. John intends to use his smartphone to make the payment.

- John is tasked with the responsibility of sending money to his son, who resides in another country. He has chosen PayPal as the method of payment for this. PayPal, according to John, enables him to send money to his family quickly and easily online. To complete the transaction, he needs his son's e-mail address.

- Additionally, John intends to use his credit card to make purchases on Amazon's online store.

- Finally, he has some $500 notes in his possession that he needs to deposit in the bank.

Which of the alternatives above do you believe falls under the category of digital Money?

Except for $500 bills that must be deposited at a bank, all other alternatives are digital money transactions. Payments made by PayPal, credit card, or online bill pay do not involve physical money exchange. As a result, these transactions obviate the necessity for actual cash transfers.

Peer-to-peer value transfers are now possible due to the advent of digital currency. New currencies will emerge as the fundamental principles underlying massive, systemically significant cross-border social and economic networks. With the introduction of these new currencies, the competitive nature of currencies, the architecture of the international monetary system, and the purpose of government-issued public Money are all altered. Money homogeneity is a word that refers to a quantitative easing technique that results in some degree of consistency among various types of Money. A convertibility arrangement is when the issuer of a money commodity enters into a legally enforceable obligation to swap the instrument with another financial intermediary at a predetermined rate.

A bank is an excellent example of an agent bound by law to assure convertibility. Support safeguards the value of a financial asset while giving the issuer more flexibility. Money pegs and currency bands are excellent examples of supportive systems. Money is divided into two categories: account-based Money and token Money. Outside Money is a claim on an unexistent asset; internal Money is cash in a bank account.

Chapter 2: Universal Intelligence and Money

There are numerous viewpoints and beliefs regarding Universal Intelligence that originated and continues to create everything that exists. Some people refer to this mighty power as God, some as Spirit, and yet others as a bunch of nonsense. If you are one of those cynical people about such woo-hooery but desire to get rich, I strongly advise you to set aside your cynicism and agree to test some new beliefs. Because not only may you very well witness enormous outcomes from partying with Universal Intelligence, but I am telling you that, whether you like it or not, you already believe in it. You believe in something. Whether it is fate, good fortune, or divine intervention, you have already knocked on wood. You have prayed when your team is on the verge of defeating you or when you spot blue and red flashing lights in your rearview mirror. You have previously expressed gratitude to someone named God or added an "Oh my!" before his name while seeing a video of an older woman skating over a mound of her grandkids. You have received a miraculously knowing hint from an unknown source. "I am not sure what prompted me to call Mom on the way home, but if I had not, she would still be laying on the floor." You have seen a glimpse of something out there that you cannot quite put your head around, something that is actively involved in our lives. You have felt it tickle the back of your neck's hair. Even if it is only a splash of recognition, you have communicated with Universal Intelligence.

2.1 Universal Intelligence

The reason I insist on this is that once you admit that a force greater than your physical self is at work in your life, you may begin utilizing the Universe's high and unlimited power to earn some money around here. We have been conditioned to accept the information conveyed to us through our five bodily senses as fact. Meanwhile, without seeming ungrateful for the awesomeness supplied by my eyes, ears, nose, skin, and tongue — seriously, folks, a giant thank you — these senses are limited. Our senses supply just a limited amount of information due to their limited range. For instance, the human sense of smell is far inferior to that of a dog. A dog can smell when the seal on a package of salami is cracked from the adjacent room. While sleeping, Bats can downright mock us just in front of our faces at frequencies that we cannot hear. With their bionic night vision, Cats will always defeat us in an obstacle course competition held after dark. While most people define reality in terms of what their five senses see, there is so much more going on, such as an infinite, everlasting Universe's worth of stuff.

As with electricity and gravity — two factors affecting the daily lives that we cannot see, understand, or believe in — Universal Intelligence and the power of our ideas are natural and affect our lives every instant. You demonstrate your faith in gravity and electricity by not flinging yourself off roofs and not picking at a light socket with a fork. You may not comprehend the intricate details of how it all works, but you are wholly committed to following the rules. I want to encourage you to do the same thing with the information I am about to share with you — to put it into practice as you launch on your path to wealth and let the outcomes speak for themselves. Because believe me, once you see how powerful your thoughts and Universal Intelligence are, even if you do not fully comprehend everything involved, you will be on board once you start rolling in the wealth.

We live in an energy-based cosmos. Everything vibrates, moves, transforms, and buzzes. This is true of everything visible and invisible: this book, microwaves, your automobile, a brick, thoughts, money, words, a rock, a peck of pickled peppers, and so on. Our five senses are one method in which we interpret this energy: Our eyes detect light energy, our ears translate sound waves, and our touch translates energy into a solid mass, among other things. However, this is merely a limited perception of reality. This view of our world is also filtered via the lens of the belief system we have developed throughout our life. Between our five physical senses and our belief system's "truth blueprint," our perspective of reality is somewhat constrained.

What excites me about being alive on planet Earth as a conscious human being is that we have the ability to participate in a realm of reality that extends well beyond what our truth blueprint, our five senses, or even a dog, cat, or bat's senses tell us. And our thoughts are the means by which we transcend this constrained environment.

Nothing occurs or happens without consideration: our astounding solar system, your favorite music, the amount of money in your bank account, and everything in between. Our thoughts are connected to the invisible energy that underpins everything and helps shape it into what we experience on the physical level. And here's the real head-scratcher: Universal Intelligence and your thoughts are essentially the same force—just as a single water droplet drops in the ocean, your thoughts exist as a component of Universal Intelligence. In other words, you are a highly effective expert.

The invisible world is responsible for the visible world's creation.

The more mindful you are about thinking powerful thoughts and the less you get sucked into the limiting features of the illusion formed by your five senses and truth blueprint, the more in tune and connected you are to Universal Intelligence, and the easier it will be to become rich. You communicate with and remain connected to Universal Intelligence through two types of thoughts: outgoing thought and incoming thought.

2.2 Outgoing Thoughts

We are the only species on Earth with the capacity for conscious thought, and we use it to shape our realities and paychecks by alerting Universal Intelligence to the fact that this is the case. Universal Intelligence has created all that is and all that will be, and your ideas are how you use your free will to harness the power of Universal Intelligence to shape your reality. If you send out thoughts such as I cannot afford a vacation and do not anticipate this situation changing very soon, the Universe responds with, Noted! You cannot afford it. I am stuck at home! Just as your ideas generated the financial reality you are currently experiencing, you can also use them to overcome what "is" to manifest any reality you desire. And by that, I mean anything you set your mind to. This is because everything you can imagine already exists in the cosmos; otherwise, you would be incapable of imagining it. I realize that bananas, but bear with me here.

Physical, mental, and spiritual information all emanate from the same source: Universal Intelligence. Where do your thoughts originate before they enter your mind? Where is the flower that sprouts from the tiny seed? Where is the reality of your income tripling as a result of your fantastic new cat costume business? All of this already exists in the energetic realm, and it is only through our minds — and the way our attitude motivates us to act — that the new reality manifests on the physical plane. If you can conceive of thought, it already exists. And, because everything originates from Universal Intelligence, that thought must also live in a physical form. If you want to make $50,000, the funds and the means to make it are both currently available to you. You would not be able to think of it if you could not think of it in the first instance, because the concept of money and the wealth itself are the same thing.

The truth is dictated by your thoughts. So, if you are now living in your mother's basement and working for $7.95 an hour at the Poultry Shack down the street, and you have set your mind on having a two-hundred-acre poultry farm and a Range rover, that poultry farm and gorgeous ride are your destiny. Your thoughts signal Universal Intelligence to begin organizing energy in order to materialize your goals in material reality. Your emotions are triggered by your thoughts, which motivates you to act, and your reality begins to alter. This is how individuals in wheelchairs conquer mountains and people who grew up in great poverty become wealthy. They believe their thoughts to be true, regardless of how "real" their "reality" appears, get worked up about it, and make things work. Instead of compromising for what they see around them, they use the power that we all have to create what they want.

The term "opportunity" is subjective. Deciding to realize about money and your reality with regards to money, in a way that will make you rich rather than keeping you poor, is mastering the mentality of wealth.

When you deliberately focus your feelings on the economic power you desire, imagine rolling around with a great big pile of leaves of Benjamins, experiencing how good and right and exciting it feels to be in the monetary flow you set the energy all over you, and then within you, to pulsate at a higher frequency, and your reality reflects back to you high prospects and things. This energy is palpable. It genuinely boosts your spirits and draws into your radar all the high-frequency chances and things you block yourself off from when you are all low-vibe and sad about your weak financial account, lack of employment alternatives, botched effort at getting a promotion, and so forth. Meanwhile, thinking about how great it will feel to pay off your seventeen credit card debt, telling yourself over and over that you are so grateful this card is paid off in full that you can hardly stand it, writing an actual check for the exact amount to pay it off and looking at it every day. All of these thoughts cause the energy around you to vibrate at a higher frequency. These positive thoughts help you let go of your aversion to receiving money — you are on board, you believe it, you feel it, and you love it! Once you have removed your resistance, you will be back in your natural state of flow, with no uncertainty or fear clogging up your energy, and the Universe will be able to provide you with the wealth you seek.

2.3 Incoming Thoughts

The Universe is always popping up with a cup of coffee in hand, eager to talk about how to improve your money and lend a hand. It makes a connection with you:

- Via your intuition:
- Via synchronicity:
- Via inspiration:
- Via desire:
- Via coincidence:

If you are serious about making a difference, you'll want to improve your relationship with the Universe by doing the following:

- Learn to calm your mind so you can hear what it's trying to tell you.

- Trust that this knowledge (aka your intuition) will give you with all of the answers you want, no matter how scary/bananas/unacceptable they may appear.

- Surrender and trust that the Universe will protect you as you boldly venture into the unknown.

- Accept that you do not need to know how to accomplish something you do not yet know how to do, and that the Universe will guide you.

We all have the potential to harness the power of the Universe via our thoughts.

I am not sure what more to say if that does not make you want to go out and get a superhero cape and tights.

2.4 Money as a Medium of Exchange

Without investigating your words, thoughts, and beliefs, you run the risk of stumbling through life on autopilot. For instance, you may instantly think that your beliefs are grounded on your facts rather than the truths of your parents and the individuals in your immediate environment. Or that your words accurately convey your beliefs, rather than being mindless regurgitations of information you have already heard, or evidence of your poor command of the English language. And do not even get me started on the amount of time we squander spinning out on, shall we say, less than valuable thoughts. Once you awaken, become aware of your thoughts, beliefs, and words, and begin choosing them wisely, you can avoid being trapped in a life of excruciating tiredness (or worse), perpetual financial struggle, or, as happened to Mom, being reprimanded for having a potty mouth by someone who is a far inferior gardener to you.

When we do not master our brains, we risk establishing our lives on shaky ground.

It's vital to master your thinking in all areas of your life, but it is more critical when it comes to money because money plays such a significant role on Earth. Without it, we literally cannot operate. Discovering you have left the house without your wallet is as frightening as finding you have forgotten your journal on the metro or Grandma at the truck stop. There is not a day that goes by that we do not use money or anything purchased with money or have an experience that involves money in some way. Money is everywhere. It is in the roads we travel, the food we eat, the music we listen to, the freedom we enjoy, the adventures we have, the babies we give birth to, the showers we take, the poems we write, and the horns we blow.

And yet, we rarely, if ever, pause to consider our attitudes about money, how we speak about it, or even what money is. As a result, I am going to pause right now.

Medium of Exchange

Before the advent of money, people exchanged goods and services through bartering. They would trade you a cart for a couple of sheep or construct a stone wall for someone in exchange for a pile of animal pelts and a bag of salt. Then it became too inconvenient to carry coats and boulders around, and it took too long to build things, so humans invented money, assigned a value to coins and notes, and today all you have to do is to reach for your wallet instead of five of your best camels to get the car or anything.

Money is a unit of measurement that is used in the giving and receiving of goods and services. Contrary to common opinion, money is neither good nor evil, filthy nor clean friend nor foe. It is simply blank, minding its own business and avoiding becoming stuck in a Coke machine. Money is merely the medium of exchange. What gives it personality is what you do with it and how you feel, think, and communicate about it. And, depending on the character you endow it with, you are either going to want to surround yourself with it or avoid it like the plague.

This is why believing money is nasty or dirty (without actually thinking about it) and reinforcing these thoughts by speaking negatively about it is one of the primary causes of severe financial insolvency. For instance, here's something you may have thought and stated previously:

The source of all evil is money.

Yes, our world is filled with horrible atrocities and injustices caused by what individuals do for money, but the offenders do not cause the wrongdoing. It is like declaring vehicles innately evil simply because people transform into obscenity-hurling jackasses behind the wheel or declare vegetable peelers terrible simply because they once slashed their finger open with one. Money, automobiles, and vegetable peelers all serve as channels for immense delight and delectable adventures, and all make fantastic wedding gifts.

Money, as the late, great Ayn Rand put it, is merely a tool. It will transport you wherever you like but will not take the role of the driver.

Numerous terms in the English language have meanings that bleed into one another. It's simple to become perplexed as to where one begins and the other finishes. For instance, love/lust, being excellent/lying and being confident/intoxicated. When it comes to the drive to accumulate money, the most frequently used term is "greed," particularly when discussing the source of all evil and other such unpleasantries. Taking a moment to ascertain the facts can prevent a great deal of disappointment and misery in any of these instances. Therefore, let us be clear:

Greed: An unquenchable, greedy, selfish desire for more and more. Another term sometimes conflated with money is "power-mongering," which refers to the act of using influence in a despotic and super mean manner. And let us not forget ye olde "corrupt": Morally bankrupt, obsessed with self-gain and oblivious to how your activities affect others or what the law says.

Here are some additional common instances in which individuals misuse the term "money":

- Everything is ruined by money.
- Money and friendship are synonymous, just as oil and water are.
- Money typically transforms decent people into monsters.

Is not that somewhat harsh? Money is not breaking into your house and punching you in the face. It simply attempts to assist you in purchasing items. Here is another thing that is critical to understand about money if you are going to go out and make a lot of it.

2.5 Money as Energy

Money is a blank slate whose value is determined by the energy and meaning we invest in it. For instance, earning fifty dollars picking leaves for the lady across the street has an entirely different energy than stealing fifty dollars from some guy's pocket on the train. A shabby chair purchased for five dollars at a thrift store may be worth five thousand dollars if David Bowie used it on his tour bus. Some painters charge as little as two hundred dollars for their works; others ask as much as twenty thousand. When you are hired to do something and discover halfway through that, you have been significantly underpaid, and your paycheck will feel like a soggy napkin when it eventually arrives. Alternatively, if you are grossly overcharged, it makes you shudder and makes you feel nasty and dirty. And if you charge the proper amount, you will feel as though you are a superstar. Money is an energetic exchange between individuals. Your job is to actively align your frequency with the money you wish to produce and open yourself up to earning it. This entails being clear about the worth of the service or product you are offering, being happy and appreciative rather than strange and sad about getting money for it and having complete faith that this wealth is already on its way to you rather than fretting about it not showing up at all.

Here is a critical notion to grasp: Money constantly arrives at you through other sources and people, yet it, like everything else, originates from Universal Intelligence. This is why focusing on the frequency of your thoughts, rather than the individuals from whom you expect to earn money, is critical to being wealthy. For instance, suppose you need to raise $4,000 to fly Grandma first class to a quilting convention in Nova Scotia that she has long desired to attend. You have decided to sell your unopened favorite figurine to raise funds, and you have already received considerable money. Increase your frequency and make it match the frequency of the money approaching you, rather than focusing exclusively on the person from whom you intend to obtain it. Concentrate on the fact that you are providing someone with an incredible piece of Star Wars memorabilia, replete with a double-telescoping lightsaber, in exchange for the money you seek and deserve. Consider Grandma mingling with the passengers in first class, sipping her complimentary champagne and getting advice on which fabric samples to use for her quilt. Your focus should be on your desire for this money and its money, your excitement about sharing something of value with someone in order to obtain it, your clarity about how joyful it will make that person, your gratitude that this money is coming to you, yes it is, and your belief in the Universe's protection.

Individuals are to money as a French fry is to ketchup: they serve as conduits.

Not only is it inappropriate for you to attempt to compel anyone to do anything, but focusing exclusively on a single individual who may or may not be the conduit for the money you seek may shut you off from the person with the massive bag of money with whom the Universe is attempting to link you. It is similar to deciding to attract the love of your life. You concentrate on the traits this person possesses, on your thrill at the prospect of being with him, on your joy at the fact that he, too, is on the lookout for you. This is your job description: you smile more often, scribble little hearts on everything, and leave the house smelling like a wedding bouquet. You do not waste your time convincing the indifferent hot man from the coffee shop with the motorcycle and nothing in common with you that you are his one true love, thereby missing out on the fantastic guy at work with the large nose who is the perfect match for you. The same holds true for earning money — you do the energetic work of aligning your thoughts, actions, and words with the outcome you seek and then giving the Universe details.

It is all about the exchange of energy. I learned a lot about this when I offered my friends a friend discount/freebie on my coaching services. Devaluing my work provided them with an easy justification for devaluing their efforts: they had no reason to rise to the occasion and exert maximum effort because they were physically not engaged. By reducing the frequency of the money, rather than asking that we all put on our big people pants and pony up, I ended up doing us all harm. These "favors" were a massive waste of time for everyone involved and could have been avoided if I had not been coming from a place of discomfort and embarrassment about charging my friends.

Because money is currency and currency is energy, when you reduce your prices to accommodate someone, you are effectively stating, "I do not believe you can grow and create the money you desire to work with me." I am not sure you are that powerful. I also do not believe I have the authority to charge what I am worth or to make pricing decisions around here. Not discounting my rates does not mean I am unwilling to donate my money and services, offer scholarships, or put things on sale. Still, I will only do so if the energy surrounding it is positive, i.e. coming from a place of power and possibility rather than insecurity, shame, or I am a greedy, lousy friend.

Money is a naturally occurring resource. It fluctuates; it ebbs and flows; it is intended to move. When we are stingy with our expenditures or strange with our receipts, we obstruct its natural progression. We place ourselves in a position of scarcity rather than abundance. Our energy is transformed into richus interruptus. Even something as insignificant as leaving a large tip for a waitress, or picking up a quarter lying on the street rather than passing it by, or letting your neighbor pay you for watching her dog all day, which you would have done for free — all of this stems from abundance energy and a healthy, happy appreciation for money. What you focus on, expands, so if your goal is to become wealthy, you are going to want to focus on abundance as often as possible. Give generously and frequently, receive with thankfulness and delight, view money as a friend, boost your frequency, and get in the flow.

A Little Success Story for you:

If He Can, You Can as Well.

How Joe, aged 40, attracted money to himself and increased his annual income from $40,000 to over $100,000:

When it came to boosting my income, I was the most significant impediment. I did not believe I was deserved money and was too critical of myself, which contributed to my self-destruction.

I began reading and listening to an endless supply of self-help books. At the time, my morning commute lasted an hour, and I listened to music for at least two hours daily. My transformation began when I discovered how much the Universe/God desired to give me all I wanted. Then I had to overcome my obstacles since the trick is that you must truly desire it as well, to the point of believing that it is already yours.

I work in a business environment, and after I applied myself and altered my thinking, I began advancing up the ladder. I took on additional responsibility and pushed myself as far as possible outside of my comfort zone.

What keeps me going is remembering why I started doing the work I do in the first place—because I enjoy assisting others, utilizing my brain, being challenged regularly, and interacting with my coworkers. Additionally, I recall that I did not want to remain in the same position as when the project began. The sense of accomplishment is similar to a narcotic.

Previously, money was scarce. Money is now all around me, and I am attracting it. I generally pay for everything with a credit card, but I always keep some cash in various locations throughout my house. Not necessarily so I can spend it, but rather to establish an unconscious reminder that money is there everywhere, and all I have to do is to reach out and get it. I know... cheesy, yes... but it works for me. It helps alleviate anxiety when unexpected events occur, and finances become tight. Overcome fear—address the source of the fear.

Money Mantra Suggestion (say it, write it, feel it, own it):

Make a list of five positive qualities to characterize money.

Every time you receive money, practice saying "thank you." "See, money adores me; it simply cannot stay away," do a victory lap around your house, kiss your cheques, and revel in the tremendous gift of being in the flow with abundance — what you value appreciates. Do this regardless of whether money is mailed to you, appears as interest on an investment, or is delivered to you by a person. Relish the sense of thankfulness and delight that comes with being in the flow of money.

Spend at least five minutes each day in stillness connecting with the money energy that is all around you, filling you up and travelling into and out of your heart. Additionally, spend the entire day sensing this as much as possible.

Leave money in numerous locations throughout your home so that you become accustomed to seeing it daily. Remind yourself of its abundance. Create an Easter egg hunt atmosphere.

Chapter 3: Monetarism and Economics

Monetarism is a macroeconomic school of thought that asserts that the fundamental engine of economic growth in a country is the money supply. As money becomes more available in the system, the aggregate need for products and services grows. Increased aggregate demand supports job creation, lowering the unemployment rate and stimulating economic development.

Keynesian economists think that consumption, government spending, and net exports can all be used to alter the status of the economy. Supporters of this theory may also be interested in New Keynesian economics, which builds on the classical method. In the 1980s, the New Keynesian theory emerged, focusing on state intervention and the behaviour of prices. Both ideas are a reaction to the economics of the Great Depression -a serious worldwide economic crisis that took place mostly in the 1930s.

3.1 Defining Monetarism

Monetarism is an economic theory that asserts that governments may promote financial stability by regulating the money supply's growth pace. In essence, it is a set of beliefs that the total quantity of money in an economy is the fundamental predictor of economic development.

- Monetarism is an economic and financial theory that asserts that governments may promote economic stability by regulating the money supply's growth pace.

- The quantity theory of money is central to monetarism since it asserts that the supply of money (M) multiplied by the annual rate of money consumption (V) equals the actual expenditures (P * Q) in the economy.

- Monetarism is strongly linked with economist Milton Friedman. He believed that the government should maintain a relatively stable money supply, growing it somewhat each year to accommodate the economy's natural development.

- Monetarism is a school of Keynesian economics that, in contrast to most Keynesians, stresses the use of monetary policy rather than fiscal policy to control aggregate demand.

- While most current economists oppose the emphasis on money expansion advocated by monetarists in the past, some of the theory's fundamental premises have become a cornerstone of nonmonetarist research.

Recognise Monetarism

Monetary policy, a monetarism-related economic instrument, is used to modify interest rates, which controls the money supply. When interest rates rise, people are more motivated to save than spend, resulting in a reduction or contraction of the money supply. On the other hand, when interest rates are reduced as part of an expansionary monetary policy, the cost of borrowing lowers, allowing individuals to borrow even more spend more, therefore boosting the economy.

Milton Friedman's Contribution to Monetarism

Monetarism is frequently affiliated with economist Milton Friedman, who made the argument, focusing on the money supply, that the government should maintain a relatively constant money supply, slightly expanding it each year to accommodate its natural growth. Due to the inflationary effects of excessive money supply expansion, Friedman, the founder of monetarism, argued that monetary policy should be conducted by locating the rate of growth of the money supply to maintain economic and price stability.

Monetarism grew in popularity throughout the 1970s, a decade marked by high and increasing inflation and poor economic development. Monetarism's policies were crucial in bringing inflation down in the United States and the United Kingdom. After inflation in the United States peaked at 20% in 1979, the Fed changed its functional approach to matching monetarist theory. Economists, politicians, and investors avidly awaited any fresh data on the money supply throughout this historical period.

Monetary policy, in general, can be classified as contractionary or expansionary. When the Fed pursues a contractionary monetary policy, it increases the federal funds rate or contracts the money supply. Expansionary monetary policy works by accelerating the expansion of the money supply or by decreasing short-term interest rates.

Monetarism, however, fell out of favour with many economists in the years that followed, as the relationship between various measures of money supply and inflation proved to be less noticeable than most monetarist models had predicted. Additionally, monetarism's capacity to describe the US economy deteriorated during the subsequent decades. Today, many central banks have abandoned monetary objectives in favour of tight inflation targets.

While most current economists reject the emphasis on money expansion advocated by monetarists in the past, some of the theory's fundamental premises have become a cornerstone of nonmonetarist research. Among the most basic of these concepts is the notion that inflation cannot be controlled continuously without increasing the money supply. Additionally, it is the central bank's obligation (albeit not its primary objective) to contain inflation.

Monetarist views of historical economic events remain pertinent today. Former Federal Reserve Chairman Ben Bernanke referenced Friedman's work in justifying his choice to cut interest rates and expand the US money supply to stimulate the economy amid the worldwide crisis in the United States in 2007.

Monetarism in the Real World

Friedman and co-author Anna Schwartz claimed in their landmark work, A Monetary History of the United States, 1867-1960, that the Federal Reserve's failing monetary policy contributed to the 1930s Great Depression in the United States. Friedman and Schwartz believe that the Fed was unable to alleviate downward pressure on the money supply and that their subsequent efforts to lower the money supply were the inverse of what they should have done. According to Friedman and Schwartz, markets gravitate toward a stable centre; if the money supply is not correctly established, markets will act unpredictably.

When Paul Volcker became Chairman of the Federal Reserve in 1979, he declared combating inflation the central bank's primary objective. Volcker did so following Friedman and Schwartz's suggestions. In 1980, he increased the federal funds rate to 20%. This method for combating stagflation (high inflation paired with high unemployment and sluggish demand) was thriving during this period. Volcker's measures significantly decreased the money supply, consumers slowed their purchases, and companies slowed their pricing increases. While this resulted in a significant decrease in inflation, it also resulted in a severe recession (the 1980-82 recession).

Britain was also experiencing high inflation during this period. Margaret Thatcher was elected Prime Minister in 1979 and immediately instituted a series of monetarist measures to address the country's increasing costs. By 1983, inflation in the United Kingdom had been half, from 10% to 5%.

However, monetarism had a brief period of prominence. The connection between the money supply and nominal GDP collapsed in the 1980s and 1990s; the quantity theory of money — the bedrock of monetarism — was called into doubt.

Many economists who advocated monetarism in the 1970s abandoned the approach.

3.2 Defining Keynesian Economics

Keynesian economics is an economic theory that examines overall financial expenditure and its impact on production, employment, and inflation. Keynesian economics was created in the 1930s by British economist John Maynard Keynes to comprehend the Great Depression. Keynesian economics is a "demand-side" theory that emphasises short-run economic improvements. Keynes' idea was the first to establish a clear distinction between the study of economic behaviour and markets driven by individual incentives and the analysis of broader national financial aggregation variables and concepts.

Keynes pushed for more government spending and reduced taxes to boost demand and pull the world economy out of depression, based on his theory. Eventually, Keynesian economics referred to the notion that optimal financial outlook may be achieved — and financial slumps avoided — by government involvement in aggregate demand through active stabilisation and economic intervention programmes.

- Keynesian economics is concerned with the active government of economic growth to provide remedy or avert economic recessions.

- Keynes created his views in reaction to the Great Depression and was vehemently opposed to earlier economic theories, dubbed as "classical economics."

- Keynesian economists propose active monetary and fiscal policy as the key instruments for managing the economy and combating unemployment.

Recognise Keynesian Economics

Keynesian economics introduced a new lens to view expenditure, production, and inflation through it. Previously,

Keynes referred to as classical economics, argued that cyclical fluctuations in productivity and business production generate profit possibilities that individuals and businesses are motivated to seek, correcting the economy's imbalances. According to Keynes's interpretation of this so-called traditional theory, if aggregate demand decreased, the consequent weakening in production and employment would trigger a decline in prices and wages. Reduced inflation and salaries would encourage companies to make investments and hire more workers, increasing jobs and reviving the economy. Keynes felt that the Great Depression's depth and endurance would severely test this theory.

Keynes claimed in his textbook, The General Theory of Employment, Interest, and Money, and other writings that business uncertainty and specific aspects of market economies would worsen economic weakness and lead aggregate demand to fall deeper during recessions.

For instance, Keynesian economics refutes the view held by confident economists that lower wages may restore full employment, arguing that labour demand curves trend downward like any other regular demand curve. Rather than that, he claimed that companies would not hire additional workers to create items that cannot be sold due to a lack of demand for their products. Similarly, difficult business conditions may drive businesses to curtail capital expenditure rather than capitalise on cheaper pricing to invest in new facilities and equipment. This would also result in a reduction in total spending and employment.

3.3 The Difference Between Economics and Monetarism

Keynesianism emphasises the stabilising effect of fiscal policy. The Keynesian theory implies that more government expenditure during a recession can speed up economic recovery. Keynesians disagree with classical economic theory's suggestion to wait for markets to stabilise.

Monetarism emphasises managing the money supply to reduce inflation. Monetarists argue that expansionary fiscal policy causes inflation or crowding out and is thus harmful.

Keynesian economics is a school of thought that emphasises demand-side responses to recessionary situations. Government involvement in economic processes is a critical component of Keynesianism's armoury for combating unemployment, underemployment, and insufficient economic demand. The emphasis on direct government intervention frequently pits Keynesians against those who advocate for limited government engagement in the economy.

Keynesians say that economies do not self-stabilise rapidly and require active intervention to stimulate short-term demand. They believe that wages and employment are slower to adapt to market requirements and direct government intervention to keep on track. Additionally, they believe that prices do not react rapidly to monetary policy interventions and instead shift gradually, giving rise to a school of Keynesian economics known as Monetarism.

When prices are stable, it is feasible to manipulate the money supply and interest rates to stimulate borrowing and lending. Interest rate reductions are one-way governments can interfere significantly in economic systems, promoting consumption and investment expenditure. Interest rate decreases produce short-term demand, reviving the economy and reviving jobs and demand for services. The additional economic activity then sustains growth and employment.

Keynesian theorists argue that this cycle is interrupted and market growth becomes more unstable and prone to excessive volatility without intervention. Maintaining low-interest rates aims to promote the economy by encouraging companies and people to borrow more money. They then squander the borrowed funds. This additional spending boosts the economy. However, lowering interest rates does not necessarily result in immediate economic benefit.

Monetarist economists emphasise the management of the money supply and the reduction of interest rates as a means of resolving economic problems, although they typically sidestep the zero-bound dilemma. Interest rate reductions become less effective when interest rates approach zero. They diminish the motivation to invest rather than merely retain cash or near substitutes such as short term Treasuries. Interest rate manipulation may no longer be sufficient to produce new economic activity if it cannot stimulate investment, and the effort to facilitate economic recovery may stop entirely. This is a variation on the liquidity trap.

Keynesian economists say that other measures, particularly fiscal policy, must be used when decreasing interest rates does not provide the desired effects. Different interventionist strategies include direct labour supply management, altering tax rates to indirectly raise or lower the money supply, modifying monetary policy, or restricting the supply of products and services unless employment and demand are restored.

3.4 Saving and Investing Money

Sensible Money Management Is Quite Simple: We need to save regularly, manage risk, purchase a few funds, reduce costs, and keep a half-eye on taxes.

And yet, it is far from simple. We commit various behavioral errors, including saving too little, being overconfident during periods of market growth, and losing faith during periods of market decline. That is not to say that we all make the same mental errors or exhibit the same behavioral quirks. However, several of these anomalies are relatively widespread – and they adversely affect the investing performance of many people.

All of this implies a partial rejection of traditional economics, which presupposes rational action. Rational? Consider that the next time you skip the gym, eat the chocolate you vowed you would not touch, overspend at the mall, and build up another round of frightening credit card bills.

Attempting to Save

Indeed, our behavioral challenges begin with a lack of self-control, making it difficult to defer gratification and result in far insufficient savings. Our hunter-gatherer forefathers and mothers did not give much thought to retirement planning. Rather than that, they were concerned with surviving, which meant consuming whenever possible. Perhaps it is unsurprising that deferring gratification is difficult for us today – and why we resort to all manners of deception to convince ourselves to save.

You may assume that as a substitute for deception, we could try financial education. The issue is that schooling does not appear to be effective. We are all aware of the need for saving, but we consistently fall short. For instance, if we are asked whether we would be ready to forego some luxuries to save an additional $100 per week a year from now, we might respond, "Yes." However, if we were asked whether we would be willing to begin belt-tightening immediately, we would almost certainly decline. We know what is best for us in the long run, but it is all too simple to delay because the future is so far. As in the sinner's prayer, "God, please save me — but not now."

While a lack of self-control is probably the primary reason we do not save enough, our profligacy can also be attributed to our poor math skills. The majority of us do not carry financial calculators with us. Rather than that, when confronted with common financial math difficulties, we make educated assumptions—and our estimates are frequently incorrect. For example, we may be aware of compounding, the process through which we make investment profits not just on our initial investment but also on prior years' earnings that we reinvested back into our nest egg.

While we have a general understanding of how compounding works, we frequently underestimate its influence. This implies that we are unaware of the potential growth of our savings over time, and hence are not as motivated to save as we should be. We grossly underestimate the cost of our loans. While we are aware that our credit cards have a high interest rate, we are unaware of the amount of interest we will accrue if we do not pay off our credit cards in total. Each month that we hold a balance on our credit card, we are charged interest on the outstanding sum. It's similar to investing, except that time is our adversary, not our ally.

Riding the Bull

If saving is a fight, investing is a war – and many of our wounds are inflicted on ourselves. Assume we are amid a stock market rise. At that point, our instinct is to be excessively cautious. As behavioral economists have revealed, humans are naturally loss-averse, experiencing significantly more pain from losses than profits. Indeed, scholarly research indicates that the pain associated with losses is twice as high as the joy of wins.

During the earliest stages of the stock market rebound, this loss aversion may induce us to avoid stocks. Perhaps you have heard of the market's tremendous long-term gains. However, we are far more concerned with the risk of catastrophic short-term losses. We despise the concept of investing a large sum of money in stocks only to see the market crash. That would imply heinous losses — and unbearable pains of remorse.

This helps explain the popularity of dollar-cost averaging and the practice of investing the same amount each month regardless of the market conditions. Dollar-cost averaging is hailed as a systematic, no-nonsense approach to stock investing. However, it is genuinely about investor psychology, assisting us in overcoming our aversion to investing and making market drops more bearable. It may be possible that this month's investment may prove to be a financial loss. However, we have the consolation of knowing that we will have another opportunity to purchase next month.

As the market continues to rise, our willingness to purchase stocks increases slightly. However, the scholarly study indicates that we will usually gravitate toward the familiar when purchasing. Many people appear to suffer from home bias, which means that we prefer the stocks of our employer, local businesses, well-known blue-chip organizations, and corporations whose products we use. When these stocks are combined, they may constitute an insufficiently diversified portfolio — yet this is the portfolio we are comfortable owning.

Meanwhile, we avoid exotic investments like commodities and foreign stocks, even though these exotic investments may reduce our portfolio's overall volatility. However, if the rise gets momentum, such unusual investments may appear less hazardous, especially if they show significant gains. We are programmed to seek patterns in the market's unpredictable gyrations, eliciting all manner of confident projections. This pattern recognition leads us to extrapolate current returns and, before long, we conclude that the rising market will continue to rise. Forget about history's vast arc. We are significantly more influenced by recent weeks and months.

We will quickly forget about the market's instability. Rather than that, we convinced ourselves that stocks were bound to rise. We might even conclude that we anticipated the rally. Due to this hindsight bias, the market appears more predictable than it is, which encourages us to pursue our current investment hunches.

Additionally, the soaring market boosts our confidence as we ascribe our investing profits to our intelligence and become obsessed with outperforming the market. This results in us placing larger investment wagers and purchasing actively managed funds. Men are more prone to all of this, with a propensity for trading more, hoarding more stocks, and pursuing riskier stock investment tactics.

We might even be victims of the house money effect. As with early-evening casino gamblers, our investment success may give us the impression that we are ahead of the game — and can afford to take additional risk. True, there may be warning indications, such as excessive valuations and cynical analysts. However, we overlook inconvenient facts and pay scant heed to statistical data. Rather than that, we cling to the arguments, anecdotes, and other shards of evidence that reinforce our case.

We link hard labor with success by taking our cues from the workplace. Additional research and trading appear to result in improved results. Indeed, several of our stocks have increased in value, and we take enormous delight in converting our paper earnings to physical cash. The issue is that selling winners results in investment fees, but it can also result in significant tax liabilities if we trade in a taxable account.

Money, on the other hand, is only a portion of the payoff. Put aside your concerns about reaching goals. Wall Street evolved as a source of entertainment. We enjoy the sensation of being in sync with the market's action. We derive pleasure from buying and selling. Trading enables us to develop an emotional connection to our money and a sense of control. We developed an affinity for our investments. We were delighted to get 100 shares of a hot initial public offering. We enjoy the cachet associated with hedge fund ownership. We invest in socially responsible mutual funds and use our own funds to demonstrate our political commitment.

Trading aggressively and purchasing exotic securities early in the upswing would have appeared dangerous. It now feels nearly secure, in part because so many people are doing the same thing. We gravitate toward popular investments for the approval we receive from those around us. Naturally, popularity is a good indicator when choosing a movie, a car, or a restaurant. However, crowds are dangerous in the investment world. If an investment is prevalent, it is likely overvalued. When everyone has purchased, there is no one left to buy. When will the next bear market begin? It's probably not all that far away.

Losing Our Nerves

Market rallies frequently endure significantly longer than naysayers anticipate. Bearish investors declare the end is near, only to have their projections shattered by surging share prices. However, as mother warned, "it will end in tears." When an investment becomes tremendously popular, you can be reasonably confident that difficult times are ahead — even if you cannot anticipate when those difficult times would occur.

When stocks initially begin to fail, we dismiss it. However, as the downturn continues, our confidence erodes. We are no longer confident in our forecasts and are less willing to trade. Rather than forecasting infinite gains, we are now assuming the market will continue to decline. Fearful of future losses, some panic and sell. However, many people freeze. We tend to regret commission errors more than omission errors. That we are losing money is terrible enough. However, if we attempt another deal and it fails, we will feel much worse.

As we bite our nails and hold our breath, we are impacted by the endowment effect, the human propensity to go beyond market values and ascribe additional worth to the possessions we possess. This is why we hold on to the stocks our parents left us. We feel our portfolios have performed better than they have in reality and that our investments and residences are worth more than their current market value.

Similarly, when we psychologically evaluate our stocks and mutual funds, we may be anchored by the price we paid or the price we could have gotten if we had sold at the market's peak — and we are vehemently opposed to trading for less. Experts discuss risk aversion. However, we are loss averse. We despise the prospect of financial loss. Indeed, we will continue to hold a risky, poorly diversified portfolio in the hope of "getting even, then getting out." On the other hand, Selling is giving up any hope of recouping our losses and admitting that we have made a mistake. We may even "double down" on lost stock holdings, purchasing additional shares and incurring more significant risks in the goal of fast recouping our losses.

It is unlikely that our stocks will be the source of our most significant pain. We anticipate stocks to behave crazily. Rather than that, we can get particularly uneasy if ostensibly safe investments prove to be dangerous. We are unconcerned with a 1% decrease in the stock market. However, we are concerned about the possibility that our money market fund's $1 share price would "break the buck" and plummet to 99 cents.

Loss aversion is not always detrimental. It may prevent us from selling at the worst possible time during a bad market. If we have well-diversified portfolios, it is probably prudent for us to hold onto our investments. However, we would undoubtedly fare even better if we increased our stock shares when prices fell rather than freezing. Market declines are a source of opportunity. Unfortunately, for many, they represent another opportunity to make other errors.

As is the case with our efforts to save, many of our financial blunders may be linked back to evolutionary psychology. Our forefathers and mothers survived because they worked hard, looked for patterns, imitated others, and were fearful of loss. However, these characteristics can work against us in today's financial world. Forget about blaming our parents for everything. The actual perpetrators, it appears, are our cave-dwelling forefathers.

Chapter 4: Self-knowledge is Important

According to the late great Jim Rohn, the finest investment you can make in your lifetime is in yourself. To be honest, you may enhance your life in various ways, like joining a library, taking a class, reading a book, learning a new skill, or increasing your physical activity. Continue to improve yourself. Make positive decisions, and productive habits will develop quickly.

Mr. Rohn also stated that, years ago, only around 3% of residents in each municipality had a library card. Granted, he said this a long time ago, but I cannot picture it being very different now (especially now with information being so readily accessible). Perhaps you have heard the proverb, "Readers are Leaders." Reading will significantly improve your vocabulary, creativity, and communication abilities.

4.1 Focus on Self-Knowledge

Immediately eliminate the term CAN'T from your vocabulary. You ARE, you CAN, and you WILL! You are more capable than you know. One of the basic tenets of NLP (Neuro-Linguistic Programming) is that if one person is doing something, anybody can learn to do it. Put an end to your limitations. This cosmos desires your success and will collaborate with you if you are willing to open up and accept it.

Anything that does not grow is effectively dead. Your mind is infatuated with knowledge. Your brain thrives on being challenged and acquiring new knowledge. There is so much information available, and never before has so much information been so readily accessible.

Take on a new challenge by learning a new language, instrument, or sport. Not only will this enhance your mental power, but who knows, you may discover a real passion you have been seeking. Begin with reading literature about how to improve your life. Begin reading about investing, saving, and other money-related topics. Knowledge is a powerful tool, and the more knowledge you acquire, the more value you can give. To paraphrase Rohn once more, "Ignorance is NOT bliss." In other words, ignorance does not guarantee happiness.

Develop a variety of learning strategies, such as fast reading and memorizing. There are several excellent educational resources accessible. For instance, www.lumosity.com is one of the most popular and rapidly expanding websites. You will be pleasantly surprised by your own brain's powers. This will instill confidence in you and give you a better sense of worth and value.

When you first get out of bed, read and study when those newborn neurons are still fresh in your mind and ready to be imprinted. Before bed, read and study, allowing your subconscious to work on the last item you learnt before sleeping for the night.

With whom I have learned a great deal, Josh Kauffman has a fantastic book titled The First 20 Hours: How to Learn Anything... Quickly! He discusses in the book how to remove redundant material while studying a new subject. Mr. Kauffman challenges the 10,000-hour concept in mastering any work by arguing that the remainder would follow relatively quick by learning the bulk of a subject's significance.

Perhaps most essential, it is prudent to educate oneself about one's self. Continue to be a student of life and gain as much experience as possible. Continue to learn and to learn some more. Take advice from others, learn from your successes, and never forget to learn from your failures.

Open your mind, your eyes, your ears, and your heart. With an open mind, you will discover the options you were unaware existed. You will expand your horizons, acquire new skills, and significantly increase your chances of finding your passion, your vocation.

Accept recommendations and counsel, but refrain from taking commands. You are unique, and no one can tell you how to live your life... "OR ELSE." Believe in yourself, in your intuition, and take calculated chances from time to time.

Locked thoughts result in closed doors; open minds result in an infinite number of options.

Utilize Mental Tricks: The secret here is to learn how to learn.

Utilize the Pareto Principle, often referred to as the 80/20 rule, to save on time.

In many fields, understanding the critical 20% of material is beneficial 80% of the time.

For instance, if one decides to study the Spanish language, they will save significant time and progress more quickly by memorizing the key terms, which account for less than 20% of the Spanish lexicon.

Around 80% of the time, this 20% of the language is utilized in everyday speech.

Each individual is unique and will tackle the situation differently. The most effective approach to learning anything new is to connect it with something you already know. When our brains associate one item with another, it makes remembering much more uncomplicated.

Conduct an internet search for subjects and courses on effective learning strategies, memory abilities, and fast reading.

Purchase a dictionary and learn a new word each day, or subscribe to a daily email with a new word from one of the many excellent websites available. It is a well-established fact that the more extensive your vocabulary, the more successful you will be. Conduct research on enhanced language!

Begin by asking questions and acquiring new knowledge. Expand your horizons by picking up a new language, instrument, or talent.

Begin by reading books on money management, investment, the Law of Attraction, and biographies of famous achievers.

To achieve academic achievement, SUCCESS!

- Look for sources of practical living tools, both past and current. W. Clement Stone, Napoleon Hill, Jim Rohn, Dale Carnegie, Zig Ziglar, Og Mandino, Earl Nightingale, Louise Hay (read about how she founded HayHouse), Earl Nightingale, and Brian Tracy are just a few of the greats.

- Biographies should be read and studied. Investigate extraordinary success stories such as those of Albert Einstein, Benjamin Franklin, Andrew Carnegie, Walt Disney, Henry Ford, Bill Gates, Warren Buffett, Donald Trump, Jeff Bezos (CEO and founder of www.amazon.com), Ray Kroc (McDonald's), Mark Cuban, Howard Schulz (Starbuck's), and others. Additionally, research legends such as Arnold Schwarzenegger, Sylvester Stallone, and Steven Seagal.

- Collect inspiration from the greats on YouTube and throughout the Internet, such as Stefan Pylarinos, Grant Cardone, Robin Sharma, Greg Plitt, David Childerley, Brad Scott, Margaret M. Lynch, Brad Yates, George Hutton, Tom Corson-Knowles, Don Crowther, You Are Creators, and so on.

I am aware that I am getting carried away here, but this is something I have been passionate about for a long time. These are just a few of the people who have made a significant difference in my life and will do the same for you. I owe each of them so much thanks, and even more.

These are the names I include here. Thus, you may personally witness these inspirational, motivating, and passionate legends. These are the sorts of things that accelerate your progress in the direction you desire.

4.2 Have a Positive Attitude

A positive attitude is maybe the most critical mindset that any of us can cultivate. Although the topics addressed are not in any particular sequence, a good attitude may just as quickly be at the top of any list on any subject.

We may begin to alter our daily thoughts and perceptions toward optimism by employing the following strategies.

AFFIRMATIONS

Affirmations are just what they sound like: utterances in which you express your "firmness." Affirmations are used to train your subconscious mind to believe what you are telling it. These are also referred to as "Everyday" affirmations, implying that they should be utilized daily! Not once or for a few days, but to incorporate these mantras into your life on a daily basis and in every way imaginable.

You may have heard that daily affirmations are ineffective, which is perfectly OK.

Everyone has an opinion, but let us simply ask, for the sake of the doubters, how much harm can they do? The answer is absolutely not.

Someone who claims that affirmations are ineffective may not understand how to use them effectively. You can repeat words to yourself all day and night, but they will have little effect unless you genuinely believe and feel them. Tony Robbins uses the term "incantations" to refer to the process through which sensations and emotions accompany each affirmation.

I believe myself to be living proof of the affirmations practice, more precisely Tony Robbin's usage of "Incantations." You will become what you think about the most frequently.

For the purpose of argument, let us assume that you repeatedly do something that you initially did not believe completely. If you continue to repeat a specific phrase, your brain will eventually believe it to be true.

Each time you repeat these excellent (or unfavorable) ideas, you are rewiring your brain, a process known as brain plasticity. Your brain is constantly developing, and by ingesting these concepts, you will ultimately reach your subconscious. Once again, you will become the subject of your most frequent thoughts.

Another sleight of hand with affirmations and incantations is that they must be spoken in the current time. Consider that what you are saying is already here because it is. You just have not connected yourself with it.

To attract anything, you must first be connected with the object of your desire. Otherwise, you will remain on the outside, and it will forever elude you.

"I choose to produce all of this or better," concludes the affirmation list. This verifies that you are acting voluntarily.

AFFORMATIONS

The term "affirmation" originates in Latin and means "to make solid." The term "formation" may be defined as "to form." By integrating the two, we can develop a belief and then solidify it.

The Term "afformations" refers to asking questions to yourself as a form of self-help through positive thinking. Through the technique of question and answer, we can create a belief with knowledge.

Utilize Mind Tricks: The goal here is to instill every good belief conceivable in our brains continually. Once again, these techniques apply to every situation. Because we are discussing money here, the following affirmations and forms will be about attracting money.

To begin, we must start with the fundamentals of our daily language. Begin by observing and altering the small things that have a cumulative effect on you. When you say, "I CAN'T AFFORD X," or "I DON'T HAVE ENOUGH MONEY," you are expressing a sense of deprivation. While it may be customary for you to perceive a price and speak such phrases, our objective is to capture and eliminate these ideas.

Substitute something simple for ideas of scarcity, such as "I chose not to purchase this item today." This remark alone will come from a position of choice rather than "can't."

Regardless, such harsh comments will no longer be an issue shortly.

The next part contains some powerful affirmations (Incantations) and additional information to aid you. Daily, repeat one to five of these. Repeat them for at least three weeks, but ideally for 90 days, to ensure that they get ingrained in your belief system. Create uplifting, present-tense phrases and infuse them with emotion. BELIEVE IN YOURSELF, BELIEVE IN YOURSELF, BELIEVE IN YOURSELF!

Always attempt to repeat these in the morning and just before going to bed. Create post-it notes and set these phrases on your bedside, bathroom mirror, or in your car, as appropriate.

Bear in mind that these are meaningless without an emotional component. Each sentence should begin and end with the phrase "I AM." Utilizing "I AM" places you in a position of already possessing whatever you wish to manifest.

Affirmations/Incantations:

- I am affluent. I Am.
- I am fascinated with MONEY. I AM.
- I HAVE A LARGE AMOUNT OF MONEY.
- I am a natural at attracting MONEY into my life. I Am.
- I prefer to have a positive attitude about MONEY. I DO.

Afformations:

- Why am I so wealthy?
- Why am I so in love with MONEY?
- How did I wind up with such a large sum of MONEY?
- Why am I so readily attracted?
- Why do I have such a nice feeling about it?

You are free to utilize any of these recommendations or to create your own. Simply make a note of them and REPEAT, REPEAT, REPEAT!!!

Chapter 5: The Art of Making Money

To become wealthy, you must combine your desire for money with the zeal of a goat begging to be let off the porch. And the way to do this is by being crystal clear about the details of your why: Why are you in need of this money? What will you do with it? How will it feel to create it, spend it, and revel in the expression of your all-important why? If you believe you can get wealthy by selling handmade ice cream, you will retreat to your goat pen of complacency rather than taking action. Consider what prompted you to take up this book. How would having more money add value to your life? How would becoming wealthy alter your identity in the world? Which of your talents are you most eager to exchange for money? Where do you believe you contribute the greatest value to your fellow humans? How does it feel to share your most ferocious self with others?

If you want to earn more money, you need to connect with the emotions associated with your goal, since emotions are what motivate you to take action. And if you want to earn money like you have never earned before, you are going to have to do a lot of things you have never done before, which will terrify and challenge (and thrill) the living daylights out of you. Thus, you will want to be ecstatic about being wealthy and crystal clear about why it is so critical to you. These are the most effective methods.

5.1 Don't Mistake Your Vocation

The safest course of action and the most certain path to success for a young guy starting out in life is to choose a career that is most compatible with his interests. Parents and guardians are frequently fairly neglectful in this respect. It is rather typical for fathers to say things like, "I am the father of five sons. Billy will become a pastor; John will become a lawyer; Tom will become a physician; and Ramsey will become a farmer. " He then enters town and peruses the area, unsure of what he would do with Sammy. He comes to his house and declares, "Sammy, I see that watchmaking is a pleasant, elegant profession. I believe, I will turn you into a goldsmith. " He accomplishes this regardless of Sam's inherent abilities or genius. Without a doubt, we are all born for a good reason. Our minds are as diverse as our appearances. Some individuals are born natural mechanics, while others have a strong dislike for machinery. Allow a dozen ten-year-old boys to congregate, and you will quickly see two or three "whittling" out some brilliant gadget utilizing locks or complex machinery. When they were just five years old, their father was unable to locate a toy that would satisfy them, such as a puzzle. They are natural mechanics, but the remaining eight or nine lads have a range of abilities. I fall into the latter category. I have never had the slightest affection for mechanics; on the contrary, I despise complex technology. I never have the creativity necessary to whittle a cider tap to prevent it from leaking. I could never construct a pen with which to write or comprehend the workings of a steam engine. Suppose a man were to take such a boy as I was and attempt to train him as a watchmaker. In that case, after a five- or seven-year apprenticeship, the boy might be able to disassemble and reassemble a watch. Still, he would spend the rest of his life working uphill, seizing every opportunity to leave his work and idle away his time. He is repulsed by watchmaking.

Unless a man pursues the career that nature intended for him and that is most suited to his particular gift, he will fail. I am relieved to know that the vast majority of people do discover their true calling. Nonetheless, we find several individuals who have misunderstood their calling, from the blacksmith on up (or down) to the pastor. You will witness, for example, the remarkable linguist, the "educated blacksmith," who should have been a language instructor; and you may have met attorneys, physicians, and clergymen who were more suited to the anvil or the lapstone by nature.

5.2 Get Specific

The average person is barely motivated enough to scrape together enough money to survive, with the occasional splurge impractical. Yet, expensive shoes are thrown in here and there, let alone saddle up to earn the kind of money that can transform their entire life.

To be sure, everyone has the ability, but you need a roaring blaze of desire roaring in your heart if you are going to take the risks, make the mental shifts, and stick with it until you reach your new, sparkly financial reality.

To motivate ourselves to earn money in new and interesting ways, we need to be enthusiastic about it. And, because money is a worthless collection of paper and coins on its own, you are going to want to be absolutely clear about what money is for, what it means to you, and how it makes you feel. This will be your fire. Vague ambitions result in vapid outcomes; precise aspirations result in assassination. This is for a variety of reasons:

Specifics enable the Universe to carry out your command.

You would not walk into a deli and request a sandwich by saying, "Hello, yeah, I would like a sandwich." You would place an order for the precise type you desire: "Roast beef, mayonnaise, no mustard, pickles, lettuce, and tomato on a roll, please — not that roll. Is it possible for me to have that larger roll over there? " And therefore, you will receive the sandwich that you ordered. And it would bring you joy. The Universe, too, needs specifics. It will react, as it always does, but if you focus exclusively on how great it would be to earn more money, you may receive ten dollars instead of the tens of thousands needed to make a major difference in your life.

Specifics elicit emotions, and emotions instill in us the no-nonsense desire to accomplish our objectives.

Consider the following examples to illustrate the various levels of emotional drive:

You are ready to become wealthy and decide to earn an additional $50,000. You consider how thrilling this will feel, visualize your bank account with all the new zeros, experience the power of manifesting that much money. You envision yourself taking victory laps around your house. While all of this is admirable, it lacks the emotional impact of something more concrete, such as committing to earn an additional $50,000 this year, 40% of which would go toward the kitchen improvements you have been talking about for years. You have clipped images of amazing kitchens from several home design publications and pinned them to a vision board that you view daily. You have calculated the whole cost of the project down to the cost of the cabinet knobs. You envision yourself cheerfully cooking your asses off in the company of close friends and family. You sense the space, smell the food, envision yourself serving the people you care about, and you feel the joy of knowing that you made it, because everything is possible. The remaining $10,000 you have chosen to donate to your sister to assist her in starting her new dog grooming company. You adore your sister, and watching her filled with excitement at the prospect of living her goal and with your assistance inspires you to perform cartwheels. Knowing you are the type of person who can assist others gives your life profound purpose.

You want to be so excited about this money that you spring out of bed in the morning to the sound of trumpets, rather than carefully donning your socks and thinking, Yeah, that would be nice. Here are some examples culled from my readers that I hope will assist you in determining your why.

The other reason for falling in love with your aspirations for wealth is that love is your most powerful weapon against your restricting subconscious beliefs.

Love is all-consuming; it pushes aside all other thoughts and feelings, even all the fear, uncertainty, and anxiety hidden in your subconscious mind.

Consider this—when you fall in love with someone, their ideas trump all others. Love is similar to a narcotic in that it impairs your capacity to think logically, to focus on anything other than the object of your love, and to conduct meaningful discussions.

The same is true if you fall in love with the precise reason you wish to get wealthy. Any coping strategies created by your limiting subconscious beliefs that attempt to keep you where you are will be overwhelmed by your burning desire for greatness. Any concerns and notions that you are going to become a sellout or a greedy fathead like your horrible Aunt Sally will be drowned out by the harps and bluebirds singing in your head and heart. We fall in love with very particular things and people. Therefore, it is essential to be crystal clear about the specifics of your future wealth.

5.3 Coincide with Your True Self

All living creatures are hardwired with specific features and traits that are inherent in their nature. This means that these activities come easily to us; they are what we were created to do, and they are the most efficient way for Universal Intelligence to flow through us. Birds must soar, fish must swim, and the guy sitting next to me at the coffee shop needs to eat his granola with his fingers right now. When we go against our natural tendencies, we experience tension, things take longer to advance, we beat ourselves up for mediocre outcomes, and everything becomes an effort. This is why listening to what everyone else (even your scaredy-cat self) says you should do is so dangerous. You end up attempting to push your way through life, which may be tiring if sitting at a desk all day is not what you want to do. However, when you follow your intuition and connect with who you are meant to be, you have power because you are in flow, events occur more effortlessly, opportunities fall into your lap, and you are energized, inspired, and surrounded by a sea of great ideas. Yes, there will be obstacles and things will go wrong, but learning opportunities are not the same as wasting your life hauling a rock up a hill.

Pay attention to the things you gravitate toward, the things you excel at, the things you lose yourself in, the things that lead you to get up and exclaim, "My foot! I can't feel my feet! "after hours of sitting in the same position, completely absorbed. Allow your emotions to guide you rather than forcing your way through a dense cloud of shoulds. We frequently discount what comes readily because we have bought into the notion that success must be tough, or that if something comes easily to us, it must come easily to everyone. So it is not worth pursuing in any meaningful sense.

My friend labored away for years in a job he despised as an advertising executive. He is an old friend who is, among other things, a fantastic performer, really funny, and the primary reason all my parties back in the day were so damn entertaining. He would do stuff like stand at the front door and announce each new arrival with a toilet paper roll bullhorn: "Here is Catherine Atkinson, who used to live next door to Jen Atkinson. Kindly greet her by praising her for her good posture." He would organize spontaneous talent showcases and jam sessions, and he would have eager visitors sit with him while he painted their pictures on spreadable cheese crackers.

Not unexpectedly, he was frequently requested to assist in organizing and hosting events ranging from bar mitzvahs to Thin Lizzy tribute evenings, and while he liked the work and did it well, it was still labor. However, he thought that he could not charge for this sort of work. To begin with, he had a good time doing it, which meant he could not be compensated. Second, he felt strange approaching his pals for money. Finally, he believed that anyone could corral crowds and deliver jokes on stage. What contribution did he make? He continued for years, essentially doing two jobs — the one he was paid for but despised, and the one he loved but was so exhausted. Then, on a fateful day, he saw a professional MC at a corporate advertising event to which he was required to go for business. Not only was the person well compensated, but he was not as amusing, engaging, or loved by the crowd as my friend.

I am glad to say that this man was so horrible and so vexing to my buddy that he eventually abandoned his devotion to can't, shouldn't, and wouldn't and began charging for his great MC (Master of Ceremonies) skills. He also enlisted the assistance of everyone he worked for in spreading the word about his new career, and he is now in great demand as a professional MC. By having the guts to follow his passion rather than his worries, he was able to resign from his terrible job and now earns money by being the life of the party on Earth.

5.4 Stand Up for The "And"

While listening to your heart and clarifying your why, be careful not to succumb to the lethal either/or mentality. The transaction is as follows: We live in a fear-based culture that thrives on cautioning us, on telling us how tough life is, on warning us how difficult it is to make money, on restraining us lest we bite off more than we can chew, on yelling "Watch out!" rather than "Rock on!" As a result, we have brought into the notion that it is better to constrain ourselves than to stretch, and as a result, we have formed this fun-free either/or view of our options: You may either pursue your passions or earn money. You are either a good or a wealthy person. You may either assist the world or assist yourself. You have the option of taking a vacation or paying off your vehicle loan.

Rather than focusing on ways to cut back, save, and play it safe, consider ways to expand, grow, and begin behaving like a badass in control of your own life:

- Have a large, opulent job AND be an awesome parent.

- Be a nice human being AND earn a lot of money.

- You can travel the world AND also run your own enterprise.

- Maintain a healthy weight AND consume chicken wings.

- Purchase a timeshare AND save up money for retirement.

While you are imagining your life as the largest, boldest, and truest manifestation of you that is you do not skimp on inventorying what fires up your heart. As if you exist in an abundant universe (which you do) and possess the capacity to create whatever financial reality you choose (which you do), and that by doing so, you will be sharing the most gorgeous version of yourself with the world (which you will).

5.5 Open Wide

I understand, I just spent several pages extolling the virtues of specificity. Still, you must also maintain an open mind in order for Universal Intelligence to give you what you require. The object, person, or opportunity that makes your heart sing may take a different form than the one you anticipated. Again, we must trust that the Universe knows more than we do, and if we white-knuckle things like, "I envision myself earning $12,500 this month by selling three additional cars at my dealership," we will block the very riches that the Universe is attempting to hand you via a film company renting out your showroom for use in a film. Your duty is to visualize your life in as much detail as possible so that you can become emotional and excited and take inspired action. Then you relinquish control of the remainder to the Universe. Alternatively referred to as surrender, this is a critical component of consciously regulating your energy in order to create an extraordinary reality for yourself.

NOTICE IF YOU ARE PART OF THE "I DON'T KNOW" CAMPAIGN: If you are thinking, "I have no freaking idea what my heart desires or what I want to do with my life, other than I'm done shopping at the dollar store," here are some things you can do right now:

Take action on your actions. If there are pieces of the puzzle that you are certain of, that seem completely right, concentrate on those rather than waiting until you have the entire picture worked out. For instance, if you know that you want the independence of self-employment, that you enjoy sketching, that you are happiest when surrounded by animals, and that you want to help people, begin with these parts and act on them. You may volunteer at a local animal shelter and see who you meet and what opportunities present themselves. Alternatively, create a business drawing people's pets. Or help someone who works with horses to assist individuals in overcoming trauma. Once you begin to take action, you will be able to identify additional things you enjoy and dislike, and a better picture of what you want to accomplish will start to take shape. Taking action generates results. Indefinitely mulling over thoughts in your head results in indecision and grouchiness.

Stop complaining about how clueless you are about what to accomplish with your life (what you focus on expands) and start expressing your excitement about filling in the spaces.

Assume you do not know what you want to do when you actually do. I do not know if this is distinct from I cannot earn money doing what I love, I am too old, people will think that I am an egomaniacal person for wanting to be a model, and so on. Roll up your sleeves, research others who have come before you, declare that you are unavailable to live your one and only life, dismiss your dreams as unimportant in comparison to your worries, and demand of yourself that you figure it out and make it happen. After all, we have worked out how to travel to space and how to create jam from cactus; you can figure out how to thrive doing what you love. Avoid squandering your valuable gifts and life by drowning in doubt.

Nobody else can desire for you to develop into your great potential. You must be as committed to building a great life as a heart attack in order to wrench yourself out of your comfort zone and make it happen. You have previously moved mountains. I am sure you have, and it is because you desire to be, do, and have anything you want. Perhaps you asked someone out on a date who was "out of your league," overcame your fear of public speaking, founded your own business, took a position for which you were "unqualified," had children, or travelled across the nation with nothing but a five-dollar bill, a thermos of hot chocolate, and a goal. Nothing can stop you when your passion is strong enough. Thus, how desperately do you desire to possess all the wealth necessary to live the life you desire? Spend some time with your heart, get crystal clear on your why, and demonstrate to your anxieties that they are not in control of you.

SUCCESS STORY: IF SHE CAN, YOU CAN AS WELL.

This is an incredible story of a client of mine, Anita, 32, who became quite particular, trusted Universal Intelligence, and placed a greater emphasis on her why than on her body. Are you serious? and manifested a total of $75,000:

I was considering the direction I wanted to take my life in the future, and I assumed that I needed to resign from my job and begin a new and exciting chapter. It was something I had been considering for a long time.

However, each time I concentrated on that objective, it seemed wrong. Finally, I understood that in order to truly be prepared to leave my career, I needed to pay off some significant home bills. Our home was virtually paid off and the car loan was manageable, so I reasoned that if I could simply pay off those two loans, I would feel comfortable quitting my job— particularly as the primary wage earner in our family. These debts were approximately $75,000 in total.

So now I am on a mission to raise $75,000!! How am I going to raise $75,000?

This is insane! What entitles me to believe that this is even possible? I am not going to find a lot of money lying around, and I am also not going to be able to take on another job or sell something for that much. I began to feel stupid (and perhaps unworthy?) of my ambition. I felt imprisoned.

After about a week of whining, I gave up on the fear nonsense and began focusing on the number 75. I contemplated the number 75. I scribbled 75s across my journal. I BELIEVED that something would work out... but nothing did. Geesh! As I lay in bed one night, I reasoned that there must have been something I was missing. I am sure I have not looked everywhere for the money. I reminded myself that everything I seek is already present... in some form or another.

And then, I realized that I had received some stock as a gift in 1999 for serving on the advisory board of a technology start-up. Hmmm, now that the company has gone public, I am curious as to its value. The stock information was buried deep within our home office files, and surprisingly, I discovered it the following morning. I conducted some research to determine who to contact regarding these stock shares. I called the management company's phone number to ascertain their value and how to sell them. I had no idea whether they were worth anything, but I felt compelled to give them a shot. The fund manager was really helpful and led me through the sale procedure. I inquired as to the value, as it was a gift initially valued at around $200.

And how much is it currently worth?

Are you prepared?

Yes, $75,000 is correct.

I was on the verge of dropping the phone when she informed me. I am still in disbelief and also ecstatic. This TERRIBLE THING WORKS!

Never surrender your dreams!!!!

5.6 Visualize Your Goals

Visualization is one of the most effective strategies available. Visualization has a profound effect on the subconscious mind. By seeing and sensing yourself already in the position you desire, you are conditioning your mind to adapt to this existence.

Without further ado, the most critical aspect of visualizing is including the other senses. Your subconscious must think that you are genuinely present, and the most effective method for doing this is through sensation. It is as if you are content with what you are doing. The more favorable the environment, the more probable it is that you will achieve your desired outcome.

For instance, if your vision takes place on a beach, inhale the scent of the ocean, hear the waves, feel the sand, taste the salty air, hear the birds, and see the distant sailboat, etcetera.

The wonderful thing about a mental film is that YOU DIRECT IT.

You choose the part you will play. You select your companions, your location, and your activities. Consider this book. Each day, before beginning, I envision myself clearly, joyfully expressing my views while listening to my favorite music. I then see myself at the conclusion of this endeavor, filled with a sense of accomplishment and productivity, as if it were already completed.

This does, however, need experience and a clear mind (which I will dive into with meditation). However, the more you do this easy, enjoyable exercise, the clearer and closer the vision becomes.

Before beginning to visualize, you must cleanse your thoughts of all current concerns in your life. Joe Vitale, one of the finest teachers in the business (in addition to authoring several influential books and doing numerous other amazing feats), teaches how to use the "Whiteboard Technique." Create a big whiteboard in your head with this approach. Now scrawl all of the mental clutter and noise on the white board. Following that, visualize an eraser in your head and begin wiping the whiteboard. Wipe away harmful thoughts after destructive thoughts until you have a clean, blank white board. By sanitizing this board, you sanitize your thoughts.

Create a vision board to help you further. Collect all of the items you wish to materialize from periodicals and books and arrange them on a poster board. Whenever you want further help with your visualization, you may refer to all of the images on this board.

Maxwell Maltz's landmark book Psycho-Cybernetics contains proof in the form of well-known research. Three groups were used in this investigation. Basketball free throw shooting is used to determine the shooter's accuracy before and after a 20-day period. Each group receives two scores: one on Day 1 and another on Day 20.

Group 1 was trained for 20 minutes each day and, as predicted, it increased their shooting by 24% between Days 1 and 20.

Group 2 was evaluated only on the basis of free throws on Day 1 and received no practice over the 20 days. They were re-assessed on Day 20 and, as predicted, exhibited no improvement.

Group 3 (along with Group 2) was only required to shoot physically on Day 1 and Day 20. Between the 20-day period, the 3rd group would sit for 20 minutes and imagine themselves shooting free throws into the hoop over and over again. This group envisioned their shots going through the hoop without lifting a finger. On Day 20, Group 3 improved by 23%!

This study illustrates the strength of our thoughts and our capacity to actualize our desires. Your brain will interpret the images as genuine. Without LIFTING A FINGER, your nerves and muscles truly gain these abilities!

Do you desire money? Consider seeing and sensing the money. Consider what you would look, behave, and feel like if you had unlimited funds. You will receive it if you believe in the power of your thoughts as well as the power of the Universe!

The secret is to visualize yourself.

You are now living an abundant life in your imagination. Create a vision board to serve as a guide. Create a board for whatever you desire. Anything from photographs of a home, automobiles, jewelry, and even photographs of money!

When visualizing, choose a quiet spot where you will not be interrupted. If possible, aid yourself with soothing music.

Begin by rinsing all of your concerns away. This is accomplished through the use of Joe Vitale's "Whiteboard Technique." Another effective technique is to see all of your issues written in the sand on a lovely beach. For instance, suppose your job is causing you stress and is always going through your thoughts. In this scenario, write "WORK" in the sand. Observe how the tide creeps in and the waves gently wash away the beach graffiti reading "WORK." Allow any anxieties to float away.

Once this is established, begin to see yourself as joyful as possible. Additionally, it is highly helpful if you smile while picturing. Make your mental image as large and vivid as possible. Include the noises you will hear and the sensations you will feel. Consider your ideal self, the person you aspire to be. Consider the various ways in which money enters your life. Observe your bank account grow in size. As though this had already occurred. Mentally envision yourself in your dream home, currently affluent.

As with everything new, practice is required. You will eventually be able to enter this condition wherever and whenever you want.

Determine how long you can maintain this level of activity. If you initially lasted 20 seconds, the good news is that you have added 20 seconds to your subconscious mind. Make a point of doing this for 5 minutes every day for at least 3 months. Take out a calendar and make an "X" next to each day that you accomplish this. The results will wow you!

5.7 Overcome Your Fears.

Determine anything you can do right now to move a huge step closer to your objective of being wealthy. Make it something scary, something you would rather not do because it is extremely inconvenient, something that makes you feel like puking, e.g., renting a massive space for your new handbag company, flying across the country and figuring out how to get in front of the guy hiring for that engineering job you are perfect for, coldcalling ten prospective clients, etc. Take note of any restricting subconscious ideas that may emerge as a result of the fear and jot them down. Alternatively, you might have a breakdown. As I did, in the midst of this session, I collapsed into such a weeping frenzy that the only reason I survived was that I did not want to spend my final days on earth in Las Vegas. However, I felt fantastic afterwards. It seemed as if I was throwing up something that needed to be expelled from my system. I felt lighter, more relaxed, as if I had been given permission to fully mature.

Once you have identified your previously unknown, harmful belief, allow yourself to feel whatever emotions arise. I mean it—take a moment to recognize and release any grief, irritation, or heartache: You are a limiting subconscious thought, you are a limiting subconscious belief! Because of you, I spent half a century eating clam chowder from a can at home rather than dining at a posh steakhouse! Allow your emotions to run wild, but do not linger there for the rest of your life. Your Little Prince was attempting to keep you alive and loved, so once you have had your temper tantrum, maintain your attention on the future, not on the past.

Once you have identified what has been preventing you from moving forward and given yourself permission to begin releasing it, begin feeling into a new tale utilizing the specifics of what you have learned. For instance, I envisioned my father being delighted with my financial achievement. I envisioned myself telling him how much I adored him, thanking him for being such an incredible role model, and feeling pleased that I was financially secure. Another thing I did, and still continue to do, was that I allowed him to give me money. I am much more conscious of how it lights him up, which then lights me up, and my newfound awareness of the energy involved in this exchange causes me to accept the money with even more appreciation and love for my father than I did when I was in need. It is entirely your property. These are your self-created beliefs. It is about unleashing the energy that exists inside you, not about including others in your treatment session.

5.8 Be Careful with Your Mouth

When I say to you, "You can't make money because you are an idiot," I elicit a thought and an emotion in you, just as when I say, "You are amazing, infinitely powerful, and I adore you," evokes thought and a feeling in you as well. Your ideas are the expressway to the spiritual realm, where Universal Intelligence resides, filing its nails and awaiting your instruction. And because words and thoughts are total best friends—they share everything, complete each other's sentences, provide support, and pass information and emotions back and forth like secret notes in high school—if you are broken or falling short of your financial goals, you can be certain that your language could use an upgrade. Just as enormous action may bring to the surface repressed beliefs, so can observing what comes out of your lips. Words are excellent truffle pigs for revealing your secret money ideas and beliefs.

Fortunately, exposing yourself to your remarks is a rather simple procedure. Essentially, all you have to do is to decide to pay attention. Now that you have committed to reading this book and resolving your money issues, commit to becoming conscious of your language. Make the following your mantra: Slow down and be silent. Develop the habit of taking a few deep breaths before speaking. This allows you to pause, consider what was about to come out of your lips, and change your path if necessary.

Another excellent approach is to pay attention to what other people say (and, you know, kind of a good thing to do in general). It'll give you an opportunity to consider: Is that how I sound? This is typically rather instructive, as the individuals with whom we spend the most time reflect our own perceptions of reality and so express the same attitudes about money as we do.

Additionally, two words that we must be especially vigilant about sniffing out are "I know." Nothing puts an end to further research and radical action more quickly than the phrase "I know." Yes, I am aware that it is critical to be conscious of my ideas. There is no need to explain — on to the next subject! They are deceptive phrases since we tend to believe that we are very remarkable for knowing things, while in reality, regardless of how much we "know," there are always more perspectives, enormous leaps of faith, and an unlimited number of questions that may significantly extend our understanding. It is essential to have an open mind and a sense of curiosity, even more so in the domain of self-help, where we frequently need to hear things repeatedly before they sink in.

Additionally, "I know" disables our ability to receive knowledge from Universal Intelligence. We miss out on getting this much deeper information when we are so sure and devoted to what our minds are telling us. We are essentially pretending to be wiser than Universal Intelligence, the substance that created everything in our vast Universe. Meanwhile, we have lost track of when it is garbage day.

*IMPORTANT "I KNOW" NOTE: You may say "I know" to affirm your awesomeness, as in "I know I can earn huge loads of money, I know I am a competent guy," and so on. Which takes me to the second point I would want to make.

5.9 Add Even More Silence.

"A wise man once said nothing," is one of my favorite proverbs. I adore this statement on so many levels because it reminds us that genuine wisdom may reach us when we become silent, stand aside, and listen to our intuition and the Universe. And they emanate from us. And that is what a great deal of what comes out of our mouths is about. Consider me! I am going to tell you five million wonderful things about myself in order for you to fall in love with me! I am going to mock myself first, so I do not feel stupid–type stuff. Words are incredibly effective at connecting us to one another, sharing knowledge, love, humor, ideas, and chicken piccata recipes. The more you slow down and quiet your mind, the greater chance you have of making strong choices, and the more room you have to catch yourself in the act and ask, why am I going to say this?

Meditation is one of the most effective techniques for cutting through the noise in our brains and finding out what is going on below. Sitting in deliberate quiet. Even if it is only for five minutes a day, if you do it consistently, the change will be so noticeable that you will wonder why you did not sit down and stop talking sooner. Set a timer and sit in a comfortable position. Concentrate on your breathing. As thoughts enter, gently push them away by focusing on your breathing. I strongly advise you to keep a notebook handy to jot down any thoughts that occur to you that you wish to recall and examine further. Before you sit, ask yourself a question about anything you are suffering with, such as, what thoughts regarding money are impeding my flow?

Visualization is another illuminating practice. Consider spending five or ten minutes living out one of the specifics of your desire for wealth. As an example, suppose one of the reasons you desire to be wealthy is to take your family to Madrid. Consider yourself there, how it feels and smells, where you stay, what you see, eat, and purchase, and how you react to the grumpy cab driver. Consider what other people will think of you if you take this vacation. Remain in the sensation and take note of any irrational ideas that arise, such as not being worthy of going or being selfish. There are people in desperate need all around the globe, and you are blowing your money on the Museum of Ham? Anything that occurs to mind should be written down and questioned.

Chapter 6: Developing the Right Mindset

The most crucial part of the journey to getting rich is to attain the mindset that makes you rich. Your mindset plays a vital role in shaping your life and how you react to different circumstances in life. Having a rich mindset is the key to make money and be financially stable.

6.1 Your Mental Money-Maker

There's an incredible storey of how actor Jim Carrey utilised his mental strength to create $10 million and a successful performing career on the Oprah Winfrey Show. He had always been aware of his desire to amuse.

He found that he had a Silly Putty face at a young age and landed his first comedy club engagement at fifteen. Carrey landed himself destitute and living in a van with his family through a sequence of ups and downs that included dropping out of high school to work in a factory during the day and then garnering laughs—and boos—at comedy clubs at night. He finally relocated to Los Angeles to pursue his lifelong goal of being a renowned actor. He explained that even though he was penniless and jobless, he imagined directors taking an interest in him and individuals he admired approaching him to express their appreciation for his work. He would tell himself things like, "I am an amazing actor, and prominent people in the business are waiting for me," which helped him feel better, even if admirers at the hardware store didn't precisely swarm him.

Additionally, he drafted a cheque for $10 million payable to himself, dated three years later, and noted in the memo that it was for acting services done. He carried this scruffy item about in his pocket for years while he landed additional comedy performances, television gigs, and film engagements, none of which boosted his career or earnings in the manner he had hoped. However, he persisted in believing, visualising himself using his wealth to care for his family and fueling his feelings of success, continued working his asses off, and, to cut a very long storey short, he landed his role in the film Dumb and Dumber and was paid $10 million for his acting services rendered just before the date he had written on the check-in his wallet.

We all can believe anything we choose and accept responsibility because our ideas create our financial realities. Universal Intelligence functions similarly to a big ear with a glass pushed against your mind, listening to your thoughts — otherwise known as its operating instructions — so it can get to work and assist you in creating whatever you set your mind to.

If something is on your mind, it will quickly find its way into your lap.

I adore this Jim Carrey tale because it exemplifies what it takes to develop the prosperity mindset:

Make a clear distinction between what you desire and what you need — What is your purpose? How much money do you want to earn by stating this objective? When are you going to make this money? Why are you desirous of it? What purpose does it serve?

With a no-nonsense resolution and a persistent feeling of purpose, hold the vision of this reality in your mind.

Fall in love with your goal so passionately that it overcomes any limiting subconscious beliefs that throw a fuss and attempt to stop you.

Have faith as solid as a firefighter's fanny and wide-eyed thankfulness that it is already yours, even if it feels like it will take forever. Never abandon your faith. Ever.

Take action with a purpose and faith that are hell-bent on glory.

Carrey's storey also addresses one of the most frequently raised arguments I hear when discussing the significance of mentality in earning money: What if your financial reality is contingent on the actions of others? How may your ideas exert influence over the actions of others? This is something I frequently hear from those who rely on others to hire them, such as actors, corporate types, plumbers, caterers, babysitters, and leaf blowers, as well as those in multilevel marketing businesses who rely on their downline to generate revenue, which they then receive a percentage of. Consider that everyone relies on others to purchase their goods and services, to enhance their investments, to pay for their cover at their concerts, or to spare them a cent for a cup of coffee. Money flows to us from Universal Intelligence via other people, which means that no one can use the old "I can't control other people" argument for remaining impoverished.

While it is true that you cannot control other people (unless by physical force and manipulation if you are lame in that regard), you can control your ideas and actions, which is what you should focus on to alter your financial reality. Those who whine and blame—remain imprisoned: "The economy is currently spiralling downward—of course. My new electrical firm is sinking! How in the hell am I meant to regulate that?" Rather than updating their thoughts and asking themselves and the Universe that things change in this area, they continue to claim that everything is beyond their control. They cede all power to their surroundings rather than accepting responsibility and altering their own lives. Then there are some like Jim Carrey, sitting on Mulholland Drive overlooking the City of Angels with no possibility in sight, thrilled with belief and appreciation that he is rich and famous.

You may either make excuses, or you can succeed. Both are incompatible. Whichever result you educate your mind to believe determines the reality you perceive. While some people face far more challenges and hurdles than others, we are all given the same choice regarding our world. Specific individuals have been reared in abject poverty, with little to no education, opportunities, or assistance, who feel they can generate wealth nonetheless. They direct their attention and activities on achieving riches rather than toward the unpleasant elements of their circumstances and amass millions, if not billions, of dollars. Some are born wealthy, educated at the best schools, and end up living on the streets despite their fancy connections, vocabulary, and monogrammed pillowcases. Your circumstances do not determine success; it is determined by who you are. Individuals have become wealthy by doing and selling anything, yet individuals have also become bankrupt by doing and selling the very same things in the same manner.

6.2 Your Attitude Has the Control

Here are some practical methods for using the enormous power of thinking to amass as much riches as you desire:

Focus

What you focus on, you magnify. This is such a basic notion, but it bears repeating, and I will since it is so darn strong and quickly thrown out the window due to our attachment to "the way things are." We do not want to believe that things could be that simple; we do not want to give up our right to feel sorry for ourselves; we do not want to give up the comfort we derive from knowing a thing or two from our past experiences.

Meanwhile, we constantly utilise our mighty power of focus without realising it—we use it to generate misery in our lives through our beloved friend worry.

Worrying is a form of prayer for things you do not want.

Because you are focusing on the worst-case scenario and all the reasons you cannot possibly have what you want, and because there are many emotions, details, and faith involved, you expertly generate more of what you do not wish to again and over. However, the good news is that if you are one of those individuals who excel at worrying, this indicates your focus muscle is in excellent form. All you have to do is to select a different direction to focus.

Assume you are twenty thousand dollars in debt, have twelve children to maintain, despise your job, and live in a shoe. Concentrating on these facets of reality and stressing out over them will focus on the following:

- Hold fast to the conviction that your life stinks, the major one.

- Remind yourself of how hopeless your position is.

- Activate fear, despair, and hopelessness.

- Motivate you to assume the foetal posture.

Now, if you made the intentional choice to alter your focus and perceive the same circumstance differently, such as: When I needed twenty thousand dollars, it was there for me, which implies that if I ever need money again, it will be there for me. I am very appreciative that I have income from my job. Because I have a job, I can acquire an even better one because I am highly employable, surrounded by love and family.

This new vantage point enables you to:

- Maintain the conviction that you have something to be grateful for.

- Provoke ideas of how fortunate you are.

- Activate joyful, hopeful, and exciting emotions.

- This should motivate you to get out there and create even more great things.

By shifting your focus to the positive aspects of what you have and desire, you can align your energy with and open yourself up to everything you need to change in your life: money-making opportunities you were previously unaware of, people you can help and people who can help you, and the ability to visualise a more meaningful life for yourself. Additionally, it communicates to Universal Intelligence your ideas about what you desire, not what you fear, so that it may begin moving toward you. Another critical component of focus is the following:

It is physically impossible to focus on one thing while seeing another.

This is why, when you are stuck in anxiety, you not only perpetuate it, but you also lose sight of all the other alternatives that exist.

Emotion

When it comes to ratcheting it up and raking in the dough, any good thoughts devoid of emotion are flimsy, ineffective, and windbaggery. Affirmations such as I adore money, money flows freely to me, and I am a badass at generating money, when buried behind the heavy sigh of as if, are a massive waste of everyone's time. Simply believing something does not mean you think it—it is only when gargantuan positive emotions are present that thoughts can activate their superhero powers and generate new expansive beliefs, bold actions, and, as a result, exciting new realities in our bank accounts and other areas of our lives.

Because we are both spiritual and physical creatures, we have a plethora of unseen forces at work—thoughts, beliefs, intuition, imagination, and emotions, to name a few—all of which affect our physical reality here on Earth. When you are under emotional distress, for example, you weep, your face becomes tight and strange-looking, and you may occasionally puke due to your distress. When you are thrilled, your pulse races, your body tingles, and you sprint into traffic, grabbing a stranger out of their car and kissing them all over. Our emotions are the nudges in the rear that signal to our bodies that it is time to act and transform an idea into a physical reality. Just like a table lamp converts energy to light, our bodies alter thoughts to actions. In both situations, a switch must be flipped. Emotions act as the toggle.

If you find yourself trapped in a vortex of misery, it is because of this chain reaction: You believe something, which prompts an emotion, which drives you to act in a way that traps you in a cycle of disappointing outcomes. As an example, suppose your preferred complaint is "I'm broken." It's your go-to anytime the prospect of enjoyment or progress presents itself: Want to see a movie? I am unable to do so due to my financial situation. Want to have dinner with dynamic, accomplished individuals who will inspire the living daylights out of you and may very well alter your life? I am unable to do so due to my financial situation. Want to purchase a miracle medication that will transform you into a wealthy, youthful and wonderfully witty person? I am unable to do so due to my financial situation. Rather than rallying and utilising your imagination, will, and I'm going to find it out because this is critical to me, oh sure I am! Despair and hopelessness put you in a condition of perpetual re-creation of your mundane "reality"—you are unable to look beyond your current circumstances, you have blocked your ability to dream, and you have chosen victimisation. That is, with the depressing notion of being broken circling in your brain, you hardly have the energy to bend down and pick up a nickel off the pavement, let alone courageously jump into the unknown. To escape your problems, you must choose to focus on anything else and drench it with emotion.

We instinctively accept the thoughts, beliefs, and emotions that we do not actively reject.

The key to freedom is awareness. When you become aware of your thoughts and feelings—Hmm, when I say I'm broken, I feel terrible—you empower yourself to make a better option, to think things that light you up like a Queens yard at Christmastime.

The surest method to become as powerful as possible is to become crystal clear about and deeply committed to your "why". Employ your imagination muscle; see yourself living the life you wish and experience the emotions that having this money and this life elicits. Conjure up the feelings linked with your money-making goal and clutch them to your chest like a baby monkey.

As James Allen puts it in As a Man Thinketh: Fearless thought combined with a purpose becomes a creative force.

Additionally, the following information on emotions is beneficial:

Emotions are not amenable to sharing their territory. If you are tired of being afraid, sad, or annoyed, focus all your attention on developing the negative emotion. Compassion trumps hatred, joy over fear, and belief trumps doubt.

Use Your Imagination To The Greatest Extent Possible

Our imagination is one of the most amazing tools to assist us on our path to wealth. Imagination is the mental kitchen in which we prepare two distinct kinds of fantasy:

The sort in which we take components from our environment and experiences and mould them to our liking: I envision myself living next door to the Nelsons in a house identical to theirs. I imagine myself demonstrating to my children what is possible by living my ideal life.

The sort in which we bring components from the spirit world to life: the development of space flight, the concept of the first skyscrapers, and the invention of the electric can opener.

Imagination is fantastic because it is not dependent on physical conditions, our five senses, or whatever our parents taught us about the need to have fresh air to thrive in life. We can explore the limitless possibilities open to us through our imagination, not our present interpretation of the "truth." When our emotions and imaginations are at the wheel, everything is possible.

Extending your imagination is essential if you want to make significant changes in your life because we are attempting to visualise our ideal lifestyles from the "reality" in which we presently dwell. We are afraid to think too big because it seems ridiculous—I mean, we can talk all day about how awesome it would be to earn a few million dollars a year, but pursuing that goal with the unwavering conviction that it will happen, dammit, and not stopping until we get there is a whole other trouble. Allowing oneself to contemplate the notion, much alone go for it with the belief that it will happen, requires considerable courage. When something appears to be enormous, fantastic, and out of reach, you must think it is feasible before you have any evidence that you could ever pull it off. Indeed, it frequently requires you to disregard a lifetime of proof, indicating you are unlikely to succeed. It is far simpler and more "practical" to scale back the ideal, aim for the achievable, and ask for less.

The wealthy are those who think that everything is possible, even when all indications point to No Way in Hell.

If you want to alter your life, you must be more receptive to the absurd than your reality.

Making money was about gaining independence and alternatives for me. Getting out of debt, touring the world, and relocating to a house large enough to entertain more than two people at a time were all excellent motivations, but what truly motivated me to roll up my sleeves each morning was my resolve to change. I desired to be someone who produced whatever my mind desired rather than someone who settled for what was available. If I had an idea for a vacation I wanted to take, a cause I wanted to support, or a huge hat wrapped in fur and feathers I desired, I want the sense of liberation that came with the knowledge that I could do it or have it. I desired to be in charge of, rather than at the mercy of, my life's circumstances.

Regardless of where you are now, if you spend time in that imaginative realm of limitless possibilities, savouring the nuances of your ideal life in which riches flow effortlessly to you, you may begin to embody what success feels like and connect with the significance that money has for you. By picturing and seeing oneself at the desired location, you begin to feel thrilled; you acquire belief, faith, and a hell-bent-for-glory purposefulness. These emotions are critical in motivating yourself to take the necessary steps to make your goals a reality. These ideas also communicate to Universal Intelligence that you are serious about manifesting your goal, and it begins the process of hurling everything you need in your direction—including such incredulities as coincidences, intuition hits, and chances that appear out of nowhere. Your duty is to have a positive, open, and receptive mentality. And to try a whole bunch of new things. Especially anything that scares the very daylights out of you and forces you to confront your fears.

If you are not afraid when it comes to altering your life, you are doing something wrong.

This is the crucial moment for every one of us—the time when the Universe sets just what you require in front of you and challenges you to rise to the occasion. Are you going to continue with low-frequency ideas such as I'm broken, as my bank account clearly states? This is the conclusion. OR are you going to stretch, increase your frequency, and find a method to My financial circumstances are transient? It is not about who I am; it is about where I am. Money surrounds me. I am going to track down some and see that this happens.

What you can and cannot afford is entirely subjective.

If I told you to go out and earn two thousand dollars in the next twenty-four hours, if your mindset was not in the right place, you might give it a shot for a few hours and then succumb to thoughts of I can't because I'm too clueless/lazy/busy, I tried everything, and it did not work, there is nothing I can do, at least not legally. However, if I pursued you down the street, swinging a sock full of nickels above my head and threatening to beat you with it unless you increase your income, you would open yourself up to the possibilities that you could not see before you decided it had to happen (taking out a loan, selling your car, approaching essential people for help, intimidating people for help, etc.). Wherever there is a will, there is a way; we choose to believe there is not one to avoid taking responsibility and doing the painful things that come with growth.

An excuse is nothing more than a challenge to which you have delegated your authority.

The great secret to wealth is less about clever planning, hard effort, robust connections, or exceptional timing and more about thoughts and emotions. Not only do our thoughts and feelings accelerate our actions, but they also provide the raw materials for the Cocktail of Creation:

- Belief
- Clarity
- Focus
- Faith
- Urgency
- Determined action
- Tenacity
- Gratitude

When all of these components are in place and functioning correctly, you can accomplish anything.

Determination

You cannot fully appreciate new regions if you remain inside the limits of your comfort zone.

The Universe will never fail to provide you with what you require. It desires your success; it desires your growth, blossoming, and shining. It is a natural rule. However, just as the emperor penguin must carry his single egg eight trillion miles through perilous icy terrain to reach his hatching grounds, or the giant sequoia tree requires intense heat from raging forest fires, or some terrifying insect must crack open the cones that house its seeds, the Universe wants to know how serious you indeed are about birthing new life.

Your level of determination dictates your outcome.

Deciding to become wealthy entails prioritising it over all other considerations (except doing illegal, amoral, revolting things for money, of course). You must be brutal with yourself because you are not only establishing a new money-making mentality; you are also confronting a slew of subconscious money ideas that you have likely never encountered before. Any gap in your armour provides a chance for your old conditioning to seize over and steer you off course, which it will do so fast that you will have no idea what struck you. You are not permitted:

Be strange in your ambition to get wealthy and in your determination to focus it happen with everything you have got.

Before you begin, double-check that everything is in order. The line between perfectionism and procrastination is fine. Get the darn Web site up and running, business cards printed, headshots done, whatever — get yourself in a position to begin generating revenue and worry about fine-tuning afterwards.

6.3 Faith and Gratitude

Faith is necessary if we are to get from unsteady to floating in it since faith is the part of ourselves that dares to trust in an unseen, untested, and frequently disproven, brand-new, and wonderful reality.

Faith is the rocket that propels you into new terrain in search of your most fantastic goals. And it needs to be strong since you will be flying through some wild landscape, much of it attempting to throw you off course. The life you are committed to making is contingent upon your rocket being intact. You are up against not just your irrational views about money but also the terrible fears, doubts, and anxieties of others, like a swarm of wild monkeys. Your faith must be ferocious, flaming, and unwavering. You must believe that whatever you desire is truly within your grasp and that you have the tools, power, and permission necessary to create it. Here is how faith may help you become wealthy.

Faith enables you to heave-ho. You have built the life you are now experiencing by doing what you can do and being the person you are capable of being. When you make the healthy choice to become wealthy, you may find that no matter how hard you seek, there are no answers or chances to generate this new type of money. This is because you are so preoccupied with how you believe the world should appear that you are blind to the unique, unrecognisable manner the Universe is enthusiastically waving in your face. Faith redirects your focus away from the past, away from your old methods of doing things, and toward new possibilities, new ways of doing things that will produce a new reality.

Your frequency is increased through faith. Instead of chewing your nails over the what-ifs and how the hells, when you trust that your riches are on their way, you transform your mental state from uncertainty and dread to joyful expectancy. This change increases your frequency, expands your awareness, and alerts you to individuals and possibilities you were previously unaware of. This increased frequency also empowers you to seize these new, unknown chances when they arise, rather than fleeing screaming oppositely, regardless of how frightening or costly these new prospects are.

Faith enables you to reshape yourself. To become the new, wealthier self, you must let go of your current/old identity: I'm broken; I associate with other broken individuals, and we engage in erratic activities together. We imagine ourselves to be X. (noble, stuck, safe, screwed, etc.). We adore our fractured clan and would never wish to see it disbanded. Instead of focusing on what you might concentrate on as you mature, faith assists you in concentrating on and believing in everything you have to gain.

Faith fortifies your connection to Universal Intelligence. When you have the confidence to say, "I am not sure how I am going to double my income, but I am going to," you believe that the route to wealth will be shown to you. Your prior and current knowledge of reality is being discarded in favour of something that does not yet "exist." If you lacked faith in the Universe's ability to provide for you, be there for you, and be, you know, more intelligent than you, you would not have let go of your present truth.

Faith instils confidence. Is there anything you cannot accomplish if you are badass enough to leap off the edge of your current world into the void? No, it is not. Nothing.

Faith fortifies your mentality of plenty — faith in the mysterious and extraordinary shifts your focus away from what you lack and toward unlimited possibilities. What you focus on, you magnify. Thus, faith equals a great attitude, which means you are going to require some more oversized pockets.

Gratitude enables you to boost the energy with which you approach each circumstance. When you express gratitude for the lessons learned in difficult situations, rather than being enraged, put out, or sorry for yourself, you raise your frequency and make yourself more receptive to getting more high-frequency experiences than repeating terrible old ones. Resentment breeds greater resentment; denial maintains you where you are. However, gratitude breaks the cycle of lowness, exposes you to new options, and liberates you.

Have faith in the fact that you and the Universe have produced everything necessary for your progress, and express gratitude for it, regardless of circumstance. Develop the habit of making gratitude your default setting, become aware of the eight trillion things that surround you at all times. You may be grateful and experience the grateful expectancy for everything that comes your way. From the good to the terrible to the ugly, from the salsa stain on your new white shirt to the salsa stain on your new white shirt, become a gratitude machine for everything all.

6.4 Decisive Action: The Choice of the Winners

The Latin origin of the term "decide" literally translates as "to cut off," implying that all other alternatives are eliminated, and you are dedicated only to the decision. People have such meltdowns and aversion to decision-making because they are panicked and fearful that they will miss out on all the other wonderful things they want to do by committing to one thing. Meanwhile, you cannot do anything if you attempt to accomplish everything.

One of the biggest roadblocks to success is fragmenting your time and focus. Determine how you are going to get rich, make the unwavering commitment to continue until you achieve your objective. You will receive a bonus of being able to do all the other things you could not do while you were busy adhering to your choice to get rich.

If you tore this page from this book and accomplished only one thing—decided with 100 per cent conviction that you would become wealthy and remained committed to that goal until you were rolling in it—you would be triumphant. Because once you decide, you get fascinated with the prospect of achieving your goal. You scout the area for opportunities, even if they are frightening. Your faith is as powerful as a bull since you would not have opted to pursue wealth in the first place if you did not believe it was attainable. You are happy that the object of your desire already exists; it is all you think about and has taken on a life of its own in your thoughts. You take enormous chances and have no patience with anyone who tells you otherwise. Consider this — as simple as changing the colour of your bathroom can transform you into a force of nature, causing you to look at the paint on walls you have seen a million times in a new light, talking excitedly about nothing else, and inspiring friends to hide behind plants as you approach with yet more paint samples in your hands. A solid choice initiates everything — your thinking and actions — and informs Universal Intelligence that this is how things will be, and it begins directing everything necessary in your way.

Your wishes are sent to you through thinking, and you get them when you choose to act.

I want to emphasise here that when I say that the Universe begins directing everything you require in your way, this includes ideas, opportunities, people, and stuff. When you choose and signal Universal Intelligence to activate it, you must pay great attention to any thoughts or significant new ideas that enter your mind. You must catch yourself before your old programming can swerve into your path and attempt to obstruct the new you. What are you going to do, get on a plane and show up on Uncle Steve's doorstep to ask for a job? Certainly not! That is absurd! One brilliant thought that appears out of nowhere may transform your entire life, but it's worthless until you act on it, and your subconscious is so ninja that it can block you without you even recognising it.

6.5 Understanding the Difference Between Can Not Do and Do Not Want to Do

Getting rich does not always need more effort. Indeed, it is frequently about working less as a result of making wiser decisions.

Frequently, the frightening risk we must take to advance to the next level is spending money we do not yet own. It is the financial equivalent of a leap, and the net will emerge, and it is a contentious subject because essentially, what I am saying is; get into debt, and debt is our society's big bad wolf. However, debt, like everything else, is a mental issue. Spending money irresponsibly, living above your means, and digging yourself a big old hole with a fear and denial attitude and no genuine desire or strategy to pay it off is one mindset. This is not something I recommend.

Additionally, I am not advocating that you go into debt if you believe that you have other options — this is the last resort option that is only possible if you have the appropriate attitude in place. Taking a risk and demanding of yourself that you rise to the occasion and continue until you recoup your investment is the attitude I am referring to. It is similar to when you want to take a vacation but can never find the appropriate time. Purchase the darn ticket, book the rooms, arrange for everything, and then rearrange your calendar to accommodate it. If you wait for the right moment to come along, it will never come.

Likewise, if you wait till you have the money, it may never happen. I repeated this repeatedly as I pushed myself to break free from my rickety-ass existence and become wealthy. I obtained new credit cards to pay for my coaching and then did whatever my coaches instructed me to do, regardless of how scary, to recoup my losses, and each time I paid off my debts within months. If I had waited until I earned the money I need on my then-annual salary of $35,000, I would never have been able to employ a coach and feed myself simultaneously. I had to take the scary step of increasing my debt, but I did it with complete faith in myself because I was ready to change my life. Taking these sorts of risks demonstrates that you are in control of your life, not a victim. It is about believing in yourself and the Universe that you can and will materialise everything you wish. It is about the person you become as a result of this process.

If you need to take out a loan to rent space for your new business or borrow money to pay for your new assistant, create a strategy to repay your debts and set a deadline for repayment. You will not achieve anything by remaining in your comfort zone. Accept and spend the money with the faith and gratitude that it will return to you. Maintain a high frequency and a laser-like focus. The demand of yourself that you do everything possible, even many more terrifying jumps to higher heights, to recoup your investment. Continue till you do.

Chapter 7: Your Money Blueprint

What is the definition of a money blueprint? Consider the blueprint for a house as an analogy, a predetermined layout or design for that particular property. Similarly, your money blueprint is nothing more than a pre-programmed programme or way of being in respect to money.

7.1 What is Money Blueprint?

I am well-known for the following statement: "Give me five minutes, and I can forecast your financial situation for the rest of your life."

How? I can determine your money and success "blueprint" in a brief chat. Each of us already has a particular money and success blueprint in our subconscious mind. And more than anything else, this blueprint will define your financial future.

I would like to expose you to a critical formula. It dictates how you manifest your reality and riches. Numerous highly regarded teachers in the field of human potential have built their lectures on this concept. This is referred to as the Manifestation Process.

T-F-A = R

Thoughts result in sensations. Feelings motivate behaviour. Results are the consequence of actions.

Your financial blueprint is a composite of your money-related ideas, attitudes, and behaviours.

Therefore, how is your financial blueprint developed? The solution is straightforward. Your financial blueprint is mainly composed of knowledge or "programming" that you acquired in the past, particularly as a youngster.

Who or what were the primary sources of this conditioning or programming? For most individuals, this list includes their parents, siblings, friends, authority figures, teachers, religious leaders, the media, and their culture.

Consider culture. Is not it true that certain cultures have a particular way of thinking about and dealing with money, whilst others have a completely different approach? Do you feel that a kid is born with their views about money, or that the youngster is taught how to handle money? That is correct. Each youngster is taught how to think and behave in terms of money.

The same is true for you, me, and everyone else. You were taught how to think and behave in financial situations. These teachings create conditioning, which develops into automatic reflexes that govern your life. Unless, of course, you intervene and edit the money files in your head. This is precisely what we will accomplish in this book.

We previously said that ideas result in feelings, feelings result in actions, and actions result in consequences. Therefore, here is an intriguing question: What is the source of your thoughts? Why are you unique in your thinking?

Your ideas are generated by the "information files" stored in the "storage cabinets" of your mind. Therefore, where does this knowledge originate? It is derived from your previous programming. That is correct; your prior programming determines each idea that arises in your mind. As a result, it is frequently referred to as the conditioned mind.

To reflect this knowledge, we may now update our Manifestation Process as follows:

P-T-F-A = R

Your programming generates ideas; your thoughts generate feelings; your feelings generate actions, and your actions generate outcomes.

As is the case with a home computer, you take the critical first step toward transforming your outcomes by altering your code.

7.2 Why is your money blueprint Important?

We live in a duality-filled world: up and down, light and darkness, hot and cold, in and out, quick and slow, right and left. These are only a few of the thousands of opposed poles. One pole must exist for the other pole to exist. Is it feasible to have both a right and a left side? Without a doubt.

As a result, just as money has "outer" laws, it must also have "inside" laws. The outside laws govern matters such as business acumen, money management, and investment techniques. These are necessary. However, the internal game is just as critical. A carpenter and his tools serve as an analogy. While having top-of-the-line tools is essential, being a top-notch carpenter who uses those tools expertly is even more critical.

I have a proverb: "Being in the right location at the right moment is insufficient. You must be the appropriate person at the appropriate location at the appropriate moment."

Therefore, who are you? What are your thoughts? What are your convictions? How would you describe your habits and characteristics? What is your true self-esteem? How self-assured are you? How well are you able to communicate with others? How much trust do you have in others?

Do you honestly believe that you are deserving of wealth? What is your capacity to act in the face of fear, concern, trouble, and discomfort? Are you capable of acting when you are not in the mood?

The reality is that your character, thinking, and beliefs all play a significant role in determining your level of success.

Stuart Wilde, one of my favorite authors, puts it this way: "The secret to success is to boost your energy level; when you do, others will naturally gravitate toward you. And when they do arrive, bill them!"

Why Is Your Financial Plan Critical?

Have you heard of anyone who has financially "blown up"? Have you ever observed how some individuals accumulate money and lose it, or how some good possibilities begin well but then deteriorate? Now you are aware of the actual cause. On the surface, it appears to be poor luck, an economic downturn, a lousy relationship, or whatever. On the inside, though, the situation is quite different. That is why, if you acquire significant riches before you are emotionally prepared for it, the likelihood is that your fortune will be transitory, and you will lose it.

The great majority of people lack the internal capacity to generate and retain vast sums of money, much alone the additional obstacles associated with increased money and success. That, my friends, is the primary reason they lack financial money.

Lottery winners are an excellent example. Numerous studies have demonstrated that regardless of the magnitude of their winnings, the majority of lottery winners eventually return to their former financial situation, defined as the amount they can easily afford.

On the other hand, self-made millionaires experience the reverse. Take note that when self-made millionaires lose money, they often recover it pretty quickly. Donald Trump is an excellent illustration. Trump was a wealthy billionaire, lost everything, and then regained it all and more in a few years later.

Why does this occur? Because, while some self-made millionaires may lose money, they never lose sight of the most critical component of their success: their billionaire mindset. Naturally, in "The Donald's" instance, his "billionaire" intellect is at work. Are you aware that Donald Trump will never be a millionaire? How do you think Donald Trump would feel about his financial achievements if he had a net worth of only one million dollars? Most people would agree that he would feel broken as if he were a financial failure!

That is because Donald Trump's financial "thermostat" is set at billions rather than millions. Most people's financial thermostats are set to create thousands, not millions, of dollars; some are set to generate hundreds, not even thousands; and others' are set to zero.

The rationale is straightforward. The majority of individuals are unaware. They appear to be a little disoriented behind the wheel. They operate and reason on a surface level of life — based on what they can perceive. They exist entirely within the realm of the visible.

The Roots produce the Fruits.

Consider a tree. Assume that this tree is representative of the tree of life. This tree bears fruit. Our fruits in life are referred to as our outcomes. Thus, we examine the fruits (our findings) and determine that they are unappealing; they are insufficient, too tiny, or lack flavor.

Thus, what do we typically do? The majority of us pay even more attention to and concentrate on the fruits of our efforts. However, what is it that produces those particular fruits? The seeds and roots produce those fruits.

What is under the earth is what gives rise to what is above the ground. What is unseen, is what gives rise to what is apparent. Thus, what does this imply? This implies that if you wish to alter the fruits, you must first alter the roots. To alter the visible, one must first alter the unseen.

WEALTH PRINCIPLE: To alter the fruits, one must first alter the roots. To alter the visible, one must first alter the unseen.

Naturally, some believe that seeing is believing. My question to such individuals is, "Why are you bothering to pay your power bill?" While electricity cannot be seen, its power may be recognized and harnessed. If you have any concerns about its existence, insert your finger in an electric socket, and your worries will immediately go.

What you cannot see in this world, in my experience, is far more potent than what you can see. You may or may not agree with this statement, but you must suffer if you do not live by this concept. Why? Because you are violating natural principles, which state that what is beneath the earth generates what is above it and that what is unseen makes what is apparent.

As humans, we are an integral part of nature, not apart from it. As a result, when we adhere to natural principles and focus on our roots—our "inner" world—our lives flow more easily. When we do not, life becomes difficult.

What is beneath the ground, generates what is above the ground in every forest, farm, and orchard on the planet. That is why focusing on the fruits you have already produced is pointless. You cannot alter the fruits already on the tree. You may, however, alter the fruits of tomorrow. However, you will need to delve beneath the earth and strengthen the roots to do this.

One of the most critical concepts to grasp is that we do not exist on a single plane of existence. At any given time, we exist in at least four distinct realities. The physical world, the intellectual world, the sentimental world, and the spiritual world are the four quadrants.

The majority of people are unaware that the physical world is nothing more than a "printout" of the other three.

For instance, assume you have just finished writing a letter on your computer. You press the print key, and your printer prints the letter. You examine your printed copy, and there is a typo. As a result, you get out your beloved eraser and smudge the error. Then you click print again, and the same error appears.

How could this be? You have just deleted it! Thus, you obtain a giant eraser and rub it even harder and longer this time. Additionally, you may review a three-hundred-page handbook titled Effective Erasing. You now possess all of the necessary "tools" and information. You are prepared. You press print, and there it is once more! "No way!" you exclaim in disbelief. "How is this possible? What is occurring here? "Are you sure I am not in the twilight zone?"

What is happening here is that the true nature of the issue cannot be altered in the "printout" or physical world; it can only be changed in the "programme" or mental, emotional, and spiritual realms.

Money is a consequence, as is wealth, as is health, as is a disease, and as is your weight. We live in a cause-and-effect universe.

WEALTH PRINCIPLE: Money, wealth, health, sickness, and weight are all results. We live in a cause-and-effect universe.

Money is never, ever an issue. Money problems are just a sign of deeper problems.

Money shortage is a symptom, but what is the underlying cause? This is the crux of the matter. To alter your "outside" environment, you must first change your "inner" world.

Whatever outcomes you achieve, whether they are wealthy or impoverished, excellent or terrible, positive or negative, always keep in mind that your outside world is only a reflection of your inner reality. If your outside life is not going well, it is because your inner life is not doing well. That is all.

Declaratory Acts: A Secret Weapon for Change

We employ "accelerated learning" techniques in my lectures to help you learn quicker and retain more information. The critical term is "involvement." Our approach is based on the adage, "What you hear is forgotten; what you see is remembered, and what you do is understood."

Therefore, once you reach the conclusion of a critical idea in this book, I am going to ask that you first place your palm on your heart, then make a vocal "declaration," followed by touching your head with your index finger and making another verbal "declaration." What exactly is a declaration? It is just a declarative positive remark spoken strongly and aloud.

Why are declarations so useful? Because everything is composed of the same substance: energy. All energy is sent and received via frequencies and vibrations. As a result, each statement you make carries its unique vibrational frequency. When you speak a proclamation aloud, its energy vibrates through your body's cells, and you may feel its particular resonance by touching your body at the same time. Not only do declarations communicate with the cosmos, but they also communicate with your subconscious mind.

The distinction between a proclamation and an affirmation is subtle, but profound in my opinion. Affirmation is defined as "a positive remark claiming that the desired outcome has already occurred." A declaration is defined as "a formal statement of one's intention to follow a specific course of action or acquire a particular status."

An affirmation says that the desired outcome has already occurred. I am not a fan of this because, frequently, when we confirm something that is not yet genuine, the tiny voice in our brain answers, "This isn't true".

On the other hand, a statement does not state that anything is true; instead, it says that we want to do or be something. This is a stance the small voice may purchase because we are not asserting that it is real at the moment, but instead that it is a future purpose for us.

By definition, a proclamation is also official. It is a legal declaration of energy released into the cosmos and distributed throughout your body.

Another critical term from the definition is activity. You must take all necessary measures to bring your desire to fruition.

7.3 The Three Aspects of Mental Conditioning and Programming

The three facets of conditioning are critical to comprehend, so let's go through them one by one. You will discover how to recondition yourself for riches and success in this book

Verbal Programming

To begin, let us look into verbal programming. What did you learn about money, riches, and wealthy people as a child?

Have you ever heard phrases like money is the root of all evil, save your money for a rainy day, rich people are greedy, rich people are criminals, filthy rich, you have to work hard to earn money, money does not grow on trees, you cannot be rich and spiritual, money does not buy happiness, money talks, the rich get richer, and the poor get poorer, that is not for people like us, not everyone can be rich?

Every time, I begged my father for money in my family, I heard him shout, "What am I made of... money?" I would answer, jokingly, "Wishful thinking. I am willing to part with an arm, a hand, or even a finger." He never once laughed.

The snag is as follows. All of the comments about money you heard as a child remain ingrained in your subconscious mind as part of the blueprint that governs your financial life.

Verbal conditioning is quite effective. For instance, when my son Jesse was three years old, he eagerly rushed over to me and said, "Let's go see the Ninja Turtles movie, Daddy. It is now playing nearby." I could not fathom how this kid could already be an expert in geography. I received my answer a few hours later in the shape of a television commercial promoting the film, which had the standard tagline: "Now showing in a cinema near you."

Another demonstration of verbal conditioning's effectiveness occurred with one of our Millionaire Mind seminar attendees. Stephen had no difficulty making money; his problem was in retaining it.

When Stephen enrolled in the course, he was making more than $800,000 per year and doing so for nine years. Nonetheless, he was just squeaking by. He spent, lent, or lost all of his money through bad investing selections. Whatever the cause, he had a net worth of nothing!

Stephen revealed to us that his mother would often say, "The wealthy are avaricious when he was a child. They profit from the money's effort. You should have just enough money to make ends meet. Following that, you are just a tool for."

It is not difficult to deduce what was going on within Stephen's subconscious mind. Unsurprisingly, he was impoverished. His mother verbally conditioned him to believe that wealthy people are greedy. As a result, his mind associated wealth with greed, which is undesirable. Because he didn't want to be evil, he couldn't be rich unconsciously.

Stephen adored his mother and did not wish for her disapproval. Based on her values, she would disapprove if he became wealthy. As a result, the only thing for him to do was get rid of any excess money above and above what he needed to survive; otherwise, he would be useless!

You would think that if given a choice between being wealthy and being accepted by Mom or anybody else, most individuals would pick wealth. Certainly not! That is just not how the mind works. True, wealth appears to be the sensible choice. However, emotions nearly always prevail when the subconscious mind is forced to choose between ingrained emotions and reasoning.

Feelings almost always prevail when the subconscious mind is forced to choose between deeply ingrained emotions and rational thought.

Now, let us return to our narrative. Thanks to some highly effective experiential approaches, Stephen's money blueprint shifted drastically in less than 10 minutes on the course. He moved from being penniless to being a billionaire in less than two years.

Stephen gradually recognized that these unsupportive ideas were his mother's, not his, based on her previous programming. We then took it a step further and assisted him in developing a strategy for avoiding losing his mother's favour if he becomes wealthy. It was straightforward.

His mother adored the Hawaiian Islands. As a result, Stephen purchased a beachfront property in Maui. He sends her there for the duration of the winter. She and he are both in paradise. To begin, she now admires his wealth and brags about how generous he is. Second, he avoids her for six months of the year. Brilliant!

In my own life, after a difficult start, I began to prosper in business but never appeared to profit from my money investments. When I became conscious of my financial blueprint, I recalled how, when I was a child, my father would sit at the dinner table with the newspaper, check the stock pages, bang his fist on the table, and exclaim, "Those friggin' stocks!" He then spent the next half-hour raving about how ridiculous the entire system is and how you have a greater chance of winning money in Las Vegas playing the slot machines.

With your newfound understanding of the power of verbal conditioning, can you see why I struggled to earn money in the stock market? I was designed to fail, programmed to choose the incorrect stock, at the incorrect price, at the wrong time. Why? To unconsciously confirm the phrase "Stocks suck!" in my money blueprint.

All I can say is that after removing this monstrous, poisonous plant from my inner "money garden," I began to get an abundance of fruits! Almost immediately after I reconditioned myself, the companies I picked exploded in value, and I have continued to have incredible success in the stock market ever since. It may sound weird at first, but it makes complete sense if you grasp how the money blueprint works.

Again, your thinking is determined by your subconscious programming. Your thinking influences your decisions, which in turn influence your behaviours, which ultimately influence your results.

There are four critical components of transformation, and each is critical to reprogramming your financial blueprint. They are straightforward yet tremendously effective.

The first component of transformation is **consciousness**. You cannot alter anything until you are aware of its existence.

The second component of change is **comprehension**. By identifying the source of your "style of thinking," you may see that it must begin outside of you.

Disassociation is the third component of transformation. Once you recognize that this style of thinking is not yours, you can detach from it and decide in the present whether to maintain it or abandon it—based on who you are today and where you want to be tomorrow. You may notice this mode of thought and recognize it for what it is: a "file" of information that was saved in your mind a long, long time ago and may no longer have any truth or worth for you.

Reconditioning is the fourth aspect of transformation. Frequency and continuing support are also necessary components of permanent transformation.

Modeling

The second mechanism by which we are conditioned is referred to as modeling. What were your parents' or guardians' attitudes on money when you were a child? Did one or both of them manage their money prudently or poorly? Which type of person were they? Spenders or savers? Were they astute investors or non-investors? Were they risk-takers, or were they cautious?

Was money available continuously, or was it more sporadic? Was money always a hardship in your family, or did it come quickly? Was money a source of joy or a source of contention in your household?

Why is this data necessary? You have probably heard the adage "What the monkey sees, the monkey does." Humans, on the other hand, are not far behind. As children, we learn almost everything through modelling.

Although most of us would prefer not to acknowledge it, the ancient adage "the fruit does not fall far from the tree" has more than a grain of truth.

This makes me think of the anecdote about the woman who prepared a ham for supper by chopping both ends off. Her perplexed spouse inquired as to why she snipped the ends. "That is how my mother prepared it," she responded. That night, her mother happened to be arriving for supper. Thus, they enquired as to why she had severed the ham's ends. "That is how my mother made it," Mom responded. Therefore, they decided to contact Grandma and inquire why she chopped the lots of the ham off. Her response? "Because my pan was insufficiently large!"

The point is that, on average, we resemble one or more of our parents when it comes to money.

My father, for instance, was an entrepreneur. He was a home builder. He constructed between a dozen and a hundred residences for each project. Each project necessitates a significant cash commitment. My father would have to put up everything we owned and take out large loans from the bank until the houses were sold and the money arrived. As a result, we were money-strapped and in debt to our eyeballs at the start of each project.

As you would guess, my father was not in the most incredible moods during this period, nor was generosity his strong suit. If I asked him for anything that cost more than a cent, his habitual response, following the standard was, "What am I, a piece of money? Are you insane?" Of course, I would not receive a dime, but I would obtain the "Do not ask again" look. I'm sure you're familiar with it.

This scenario would play out for approximately a year or two, or until the properties are eventually sold. We would be rolling in dough at that point. My father became a different guy all of a sudden. He would be cheerful, friendly, and extraordinarily giving. He would come over and inquire as to whether I needed a few dollars. I considered returning his look, but I was not that foolish, so I simply muttered, "Sure, Dad, thanks," and rolled my eyes.

Life was exemplary until the dreaded day when he would return home and declare, "I discovered an excellent plot of property. We are going to rebuild." I vividly recall responding, "Great, Dad, best of luck," as my heart sunk at the prospect of another fight.

This pattern persisted from the time I can recall, around the age of six, until I moved out of my parents' house permanently at the age of twenty-one. Then it came to a halt, or so I believed.

I graduated from high school at the age of twenty-one and became, you guessed it, a builder. I then ventured into a variety of other project-based companies. I would make a modest fortune for some weird reason but would soon find myself penniless. I would start a new business and feel I was back on top of the world, only to crash a year later.

This cycle continued for nearly ten years until I recognized that perhaps the issue was not the sort of business I chose, the partners I decided, the staff I had, the health of the economy, or my decision to take time off and relax when business was good. I eventually realized that perhaps, just perhaps, I was unknowingly recreating my father's income cycle of ups and downs.

All I can say is that I am thankful that I have discovered what you are learning in this book and was able to recondition myself away from the "yo-yo" approach and toward a continuously rising income. Today, the desire to change while things are going well (and therefore undermine myself) persists. However, another file in my mind now sees this sensation and says, "Thank you for sharing; now let's go back to work."

Another example comes from one of my Orlando, Florida, lectures. As is customary, individuals filed up to the stage one by one to obtain an autograph and to say hello or thank you or anything. I will never forget one elderly guy who approached me weeping. He was gasping for air and wiping away his tears with his sleeve. I inquired as to what was wrong. As he stated, "I am sixty-three years old and have been reading books and attending seminars since the invention of these activities. I have watched and heard every speaker and put all they taught into practice. I have experimented with stocks and real estate, as well as been involved in over a dozen different enterprises. I returned to university and earned an MBA. I possess more knowledge than ten ordinary guys, yet I have never achieved financial success. I would always get off to a good start but come up empty, and for all those years, I had no idea why. I assumed that I was simply stupid until now.

"Finally, after listening to you and going through the procedure, everything becomes clear. Nothing is wrong with me. I just had my father's financial blueprint lodged in my mind, and that has been my enemy. My father lived through the Great Depression. Each day, he would attempt to find work or sell items but would return home empty-handed. I wish I had a better understanding of modelling and money trends 40 years ago. What a waste of time and effort all of this education and expertise has been." He began to sob even more fervently.

I said, "Your knowledge is not a waste of time in any manner! It has just been latent, waiting in the mind bank until the right moment to manifest. After developing a success blueprint,' everything you have ever studied will become applicable, and you will soar to success."

For the majority of us, when we hear the truth, we immediately recognize it. He began to relax and reintroduced deep breathing. Then his face lit up with a broad grin. He hugged me tightly and said, "Thank you, thank you, thank you." When I last spoke with him, business was booming: he had amassed more fortune in the prior eighteen months than in the previous eighteen years combined. It's fantastic!

Again, you can have all the information and talents in the world, but if your financial "blueprint" is not set up for success, you are doomed.

We frequently have seminar attendees whose parents served in World War II or endured the Depression. These individuals are commonly taken aback when discovering how much their parents' experiences shaped their financial ideas and behaviours. Specific individuals overspend because "you might easily lose all of your money, so you might as well enjoy it while you still have it." Others take the reverse approach, hoarding their money to "save for a rainy day."

A word of wisdom: While saving for a rainy day may seem prudent, it might result in significant issues. The power of purpose is one of the ideas we teach. What are you going to purchase if you save your money for a rainy day? Days of rain! Put an end to that. Rather than saving for a rainy day, save for a happy day or the day you achieve financial independence. Then, by the law of intention, that is precisely what you will receive.

We have previously said that most of us are financially identical to one or both parents, but there is also a flip side to the coin. Some of us wind up being opposed to one or both of our parents. Why would it be the case? Are the terms "anger" and "rebellion" familiar to you? In a nutshell, it depends on how enraged you were with them.

Unfortunately, as little children, we cannot say to our parents, "Please have a seat, Mom and Dad. I would want to speak with you about something. I am not a fan of the way you manage your money or, for that matter, your life, and as a result, when I become an adult, I want to handle things differently. I hope this makes sense. Now, have a good night's sleep and have nice dreams."

No, no, no, that is not the case. Rather than that, when our buttons are pressed, we tend to panic out, and what comes out sounds more like "I despise you." I will never be as good as you. When I grow up, I intend to be wealthy. Then, whether you like it or not, I will get anything I want." Then we go to our bedroom, slam the door, and begin pounding our pillows or whatever else is available to us as a means of expressing our displeasure.

Many people who originate from impoverished backgrounds become enraged and rebellious as a result. Frequently, they either go out and make money or have the drive to do so. There is, however, one minor glitch, which is an enormous burp. Whether such individuals become wealthy or labour themselves to death attempting to achieve achievement, they are rarely satisfied. Why? Because anger and resentment are at the foundation of their riches and drive for money. As a result, cash and anger become inextricably intertwined in their brains, and the more money they have or aspire for, the angrier they become.

Finally, the higher self declares, "I'm sick of being enraged and anxious. I simply want to be calm and content." As a result, they consult the same mind that formed the link for advice on how to handle the issue. To which their minds respond, "If you want to overcome your anger, you are going to have to overcome your financial situation." Indeed, they do. They unintentionally dispose of their money.

They either overspend, make bad investment choices, or suffer a financially catastrophic divorce, or they sabotage their success in various ways. However, this is irrelevant, as these people are now content. Right? Wrong! Things have gotten worse since they are now not just furious but broken and angry. They disposed of the incorrect item!

They disposed of the money rather than the fury, the fruit rather than the source. Meanwhile, the actual issue is, and has always been, their enmity with their parents. And they will never be genuinely happy or tranquil until their wrath is handled, regardless of how much money they have or do not have.

It is critical to have a cause or drive for earning money or valuable achievement. If your desire for money or achievement stems from an unsupportive source, such as fear, wrath, or the need to "prove" oneself, money will never offer you happiness.

If your incentive for money or achievement stems from an unsupportive source, such as fear, money will never offer you happiness.

Why? Because money cannot be used to resolve any of these concerns. Consider fear. During my workshops, I question the audience, "How many of you would attribute your success to fear?" Few raised their hands. However, I followed up with the question, "How many of you would name security as a primary incentive for success?" Almost everyone raised their hand. However, take note that the same thing drives both security and fear. Security is sought as a result of insecurity, which is based on dread.

Thus, will more money relieve fear? You desire! However, the answer is not. Why? Because money is not the issue, fear is. What is worse, fear is not an issue; it is a habit. Thus, increasing our money will simply alter the nature of our dread. When we were impoverished, we were almost certainly terrified we would never make it or have enough. Once we get it, our anxiety typically shifts to "What if I lose all I have worked for?" or "Everyone will want what I have," or "I'm going to get slapped with taxes." Until we address the underlying cause of this problem and eradicate fear, no amount of money will help.

Of all, most of us would rather worry about having money and losing it than not having it at all, but neither of these options is particularly enlightened.

You are unaware it is controlling you. You describe yourself as a high achiever, a hard worker, and a driven individual, and all of these characteristics are acceptable. The only remaining question is why. What is the underlying engine that powers all of this?

For those determined to show their worth, no amount of money can alleviate the anguish of the inner wound that renders everything and everyone in their lives "insufficient." No amount of money, or anything else, can ever be sufficient for those who believe they are not good enough.

Again, it is all up to you. Bear in mind that your inner world is a reflection of your outer environment. If you feel you lack sufficient resources, you will support that perception and produce the reality of insufficient resources. On the other side, if you think you have plenty, that belief will be validated, and you will manifest lots of plenty. Why? Because "abundance" will serve as your foundation, which will subsequently evolve into your natural state of being.

By disassociating your money drive from anger, fear, and the need to prove yourself, you may establish new connections for generating money via purpose, contribution, and joy. This way, you will never have to spend your money to be happy.

Being a rebel or going against your parents is not necessarily a bad thing. On the other hand, if you were a rebel (which is frequently the case with second-born children) and your parents had bad money habits, it is probably a good thing you are the polar opposite of them. On the other hand, if your parents were prosperous and you rebelled against them, you may find yourself in significant financial trouble.

In any case, it is critical to understand how your approach to money connects to one or both of your parents' financial situations.

Specific Incidents

Specific incidents are the third primary method in which we are influenced. What did you encounter as a child when it came to money, riches, and wealthy people? These experiences are critical because they shape the beliefs — or, more precisely, the illusions — by which you currently live.

Allow me to illustrate. The Millionaire Mind Intensive Seminar was attended by a lady who previously worked as an operating-room nurse. Josey earned a good living, but she always spent everything. When we delved a bit more, she disclosed that she recalled being in a Chinese restaurant with her parents and sister when she was eleven years old. Her mother and father were embroiled in yet another nasty dispute over money. Her father sprang up, screamed, and slammed his hands against the table. She recalled him becoming crimson, then blue and then collapsing to the floor due to a heart attack. She was a member of her high school's swim team and received CPR training, which she delivered unsuccessfully. Her father died as she was holding him.

As a result, Josey's mind associated money with agony from that day forward. It is unsurprising, therefore, that, as an adult, she unconsciously disposed of all her money in an attempt to alleviate her sorrow. Additionally, it is worth noting that she became a nurse. Why? Is it conceivable she was still attempting to save her father?

Throughout the training, we assisted Josey in identifying and revising her previous money blueprint. Today, she is well on her road to financial independence. Additionally, she is no longer a nurse. Not that she was dissatisfied with her work. It is simply that she chose to nurse for the wrong reasons. She is now a financial advisor, continuing to assist individuals, but this time one-on-one, in comprehending how their prior programming affects every area of their economic life.

Allow me to illustrate another incident, one that is more specific. When my wife was eight years old, she would hear the ice cream truck's clanging bells as it drove down the street. She would go to her mother and beg for a cent. Her mother would respond, "I am sorry, darling, but I am out of money. Inquire of Dad. Dad has amassed the real money." My wife would then inquire with her father. He would hand her a quarter, she would get her ice cream cone, and she would be content.

The identical incident would recur week after week. What did my wife learn about money in the end?

To begin with, males have all the money. So what do you suppose she expected of me when we married? That is correct: money. And, I'll tell you what, she was no longer requesting quarters! She had graduated in some mysterious way.

Second, she discovered that women lack money. If her mother (the deity) did not have money, this is clearly how she should be. To demonstrate her commitment to that way of being, she would instinctively spend all her money. She was also highly exact. If you handed her $100, she would spend it immediately. If you handed her $200, she would spend it immediately. If you give her $500, she will spend that amount, and if you give her $1,000, she will spend that amount. Then she enrolled in one of my classes and learnt everything there is to know about leverage. I paid her two thousand dollars, and she spent ten thousand dollars! "No, honey," I attempted to explain, "leveraging implies that we are meant to obtain the ten thousand dollars, not waste it." It was simply not sinking in.

We never quarrelled over anything except money. It came dangerously close to costing us our marriage. What we did not realize at the time was that the meanings we each ascribed to money were opposed. Money, to my wife, represented instant gratification (as in enjoying her ice cream). On the other hand, I grew up believing that money was intended to be acquired to achieve liberty.

To my mind, whenever my wife spent money, she was not just wasting money; she was squandering our future liberty. And, as far as she was concerned, if I restrained her from spending, I was robbing her of life's joy.

We were fortunate to have learnt how to update each of our money plans and, more significantly, build a third money blueprint tailored to the partnership.

According to statistics, money is the primary reason for marital breakdowns. The primary source of conflict between individuals over money is not the money itself but the misalignment of their "blueprints." It makes no difference how much money you have or lack. If your blueprint does not fit the individual with whom you interact, you may have significant difficulties. This is true for married couples, dating couples, families, and even work partners. The critical point to remember is that you are working with blueprints, not money. Once you understand someone's financial blueprint, you may interact with them in a way that benefits both of you. You may begin by recognizing that your partner's financial records are unlikely to be identical to yours. Rather than becoming enraged, embrace understanding. Make money to ascertain your partner's priorities in the economic realm and their motives and worries. This way, you will deal with the roots rather than the fruits and have a better chance of success.

One of the most critical things you will learn if you choose to learn more about money is how to detect your partner's money blueprint and how to work together to develop a brand-new blueprint that will help you both achieve your goals. It is a true blessing to do so since it eliminates one of the primary sources of discomfort for the majority of individuals.

Here is a simple activity that you may practise with a partner. Settle in and explore the background each of you brings to your money thoughts — what you heard as a child, what was modelled in your family, and any emotional incidents that occurred. Additionally, discover what money means to your relationship. Is it pleasure, liberty, security, or status that you seek? This will aid you in determining each other's present financial blueprint and may assist you in deciding why you are at odds in this area.

Then, not as individuals, but as a couple, share what you desire today. Decide and agree on your overall financial and success objectives and attitudes. Then, make a list of the attitudes and behaviours that you and your partner have decided to live by and write them down. Post them on the wall, and if there is ever a disagreement, gently, very gently remind each other of what you agreed together when you were both objectives, unemotional, and free of your old money plans.

So What Is the Objective of Your Money Blueprint?

Now is the moment to address the "million dollars" question. What is your present money and success blueprint, and how is it unconsciously guiding you toward specific outcomes?

Are you destined for financial success, mediocrity, or failure? Are you wired to strive or to relax when it comes to money? Are you determined to work hard for your money or to maintain a healthy work-life balance?

Are you conditioned to earn a steady salary or a fluctuating income? You are familiar with the phrase: "At first you have it, then you do not, then you do." It always looks as though the causes of these abrupt changes originate in the outside world.

Again, your financial blueprint will dictate your financial — and even personal — life. If you are a woman with a low financial blueprint, chances are you will attract a guy who has a low financial blueprint as well, allowing you to remain in your financial "comfort zone" and confirm your blueprint. If you are a man who is set on low, the likelihood is that you will attract a woman who is a spender and will spend all of your money for you to remain in your financial "comfort zone" and confirm your blueprint.

Examining your outcomes is one of the most apparent methods to determine whether your financial blueprint is on target. Take a look at your bank statement. Consider your income. Examine your net wealth. Consider your investment success. Consider the success of your business. Consider whether you are a spender or a saver. Consider how effectively you handle your money. Consider your consistency or inconsistency. Consider how diligently you work for your money. Consider your financial ties.

Your blueprint functions similarly to a thermostat. If the room temperature is seventy-two degrees, the likelihood is that the thermostat is also set at seventy-two degrees. This is when things become interesting. Is it conceivable that, with the window open and the weather outside being chilly, the temperature in the room might fall below 65 degrees? Of indeed, but what will ultimately transpire? The thermostat will activate and return the temperature to seventy-two degrees.

Additionally, is it conceivable that, with the window open and the outside temperature high, the temperature in the room might reach seventy-seven degrees? True, that is possible, but what will ultimately happen? The thermostat will activate and return the temperature to seventy-two degrees.

The only method to modify the room's temperature permanently is to reset the thermostat. Similarly, the only way to "permanently" alter your degree of financial success is to reset your financial thermostat, also known as your money blueprint.

The only method to modify the room's temperature permanently is to reset the thermostat. Similarly, the only way to "permanently" alter your degree of financial success is to reset your financial thermostat.

You are free to experiment with anything and everything else. You may expand your business expertise by working in marketing, sales, negotiations, and management. You may earn a living as a real estate or stock market specialist. Each of these is an incredible "tool." However, without an inner "toolbox" large and robust enough to generate and retain enormous sums of money, all the tools in the world will be ineffective.

Once again, it's straightforward arithmetic: "Your income can rise solely in proportion to your efforts."

Whether lucky or terrible, your unique money and success blueprint will often follow you for the rest of your life — unless you recognize and modify it.

Bear in mind that the primary component of any transformation is awareness. Self-monitor, become mindful of your thoughts, worries, beliefs, habits, behaviours, and even inactions. Put yourself under a magnifying glass. Self-study.

The majority of us believe that we live our lives freely. Usually not! Even if we are truly enlightened, we may make a few choices that represent our present-moment awareness during an average day. However, for the most part, we behave like robots, operating on autopilot and guided by our prior programming and established habits. That is when consciousness enters the picture. Consciousness keeps track of your thoughts and behaviours so that you can live in the current moment with genuine choice rather than being controlled by programming from the past.

Consciousness keeps track of your thoughts and behaviours so that you can live in the current moment with genuine choice rather than being controlled by programming from the past.

By gaining consciousness, we may live from our present selves rather than our past selves. This enables us to respond correctly to situations, drawing on the entire range and potential of our abilities and talents rather than reacting poorly to events motivated by prior anxieties and insecurities.

When you become awake, you can see your programming for what it is: a recording of information you received and believed in the past when you were too immature to understand any better. As you can see, this conditioning does not define who you are but rather who you have learnt to be. As you can see, you are the "recording" rather than the "recorder." You are not the glass's "content," but the "glass" itself. You are the hardware, not the software.

While genetics and spirituality both have a part, most of what moulds you come from other people's ideas and facts. As I previously stated, beliefs are not always accurate or untrue, right or wrong. Still, regardless of their validity, beliefs are just ideas passed down from generation to generation until they reach you. With this knowledge, you can deliberately choose to discard any belief or way of being that is incompatible with your wealth and replace it with one that is.

We teach in our classes that "no notion lives rent-free in your brain." Each idea you have will either be a cost or an investment. It will either move you toward or away from pleasure and prosperity. It has the potential to either empower or disempower you. That is why you must make sound judgments about your ideas and views.

Recognize that your thoughts and opinions do not define you and are not necessarily associated with you. As valuable as you perceive them, they are only as significant as you give them. Nothing has significance until you give it meaning.

Remember how I stated at the beginning of this book that you should not believe a word I said. If you genuinely want to succeed in life, you should not trust a word you say. And if you desire immediate enlightenment, disregard all your thoughts.

Meanwhile, if you are like most people, you are going to believe something, so why not acquire beliefs that support your views? Bear in mind that ideas result in feelings, which result in actions, which result in consequences. You may choose to think and act like wealthy people and so get wealthy results.

Chapter 8: Save

I believe that the concept of saving should be included in this book. There is a plethora of topics we could discuss under this topic. As a result of writing this book, we hope to create a firm foundation and inculcate basic yet efficient money-saving behaviors in our readers. Habits that we may begin right away!

8.1 Why is Saving Important

Give me a choice between a few astute investors and a few disciplined savers, and I'd always choose the savers.

The reality is that dedicated savers may contribute far more to a portfolio's development. Assume our savers save aside 20% of their annual income. That would put them well ahead of their fellow Americans, who saved dangerously close to nothing as a nation. By comparison, if a group of stock mutual fund managers consistently outperformed the market averages by one or two percentage points per year over a decade, the managers would almost certainly be lauded as market-beating heroes. Nonetheless, the margin of victory is insignificant—and the true heroes would be our conscientious savers.

Additionally, a sizable quantity must be invested for the stock fund managers' achievement to be meaningful in terms of dollars and cents. That, once again, is the domain of our devoted savers. This is not a case of which came first, the chicken or the egg.

Naturally, the necessity of saving does not come as a surprise. The majority of us are aware that we should be saving more money. We have various vital goals, including saving for a down payment on a house, supporting our children's college, and affording our retirement. Despite this, we struggle to knuckle down and save money.

Indeed, strangely, a significant income rise toward the end of our employment might make retirement more difficult. As our income increase, our quality of life tends to rise as well. This means we will need a more significant nest fund to sustain our current standard of living in retirement. The issue is that before receiving the rise, we were likely saving as if we were replicating a more modest lifestyle. As a result, to maintain our new, higher quality of living after retirement, we must either save significantly more each month or delay retirement by a few years.

When Social Security retirement benefits are included, the statistics might be particularly frightening. Social Security may go a long way toward assisting seniors with maintaining their former quality of life at decreased income levels. However, as income levels rise, Social Security becomes increasingly irrelevant — and individuals require a mountain of savings to recreate their preretirement lifestyle.

All of this begs the following question: If saving money is essential to investing success and there are several reasonable reasons to do so, why is there so little of it? Once again, we may lay the blame at the feet of our cave-dwelling forefathers. They had no intention of deferring pleasure. They did not need self-control. Rather than that, they promptly devoured what they had "earned."

Today, self-control is necessary. However, as most of us can attest, it is a rare commodity. We tend to consume excessively, exercise insufficiently, and overspend. To combat these inclinations, we must devise strategies for deceiving, cajoling, and coercing ourselves into doing the correct thing.

For example, we may push ourselves to save by enrolling in our employer's 401 (k) plan, which automatically deducts money from our paychecks before we have an opportunity to spend it. Additionally, we may enroll in automated mutual fund investing programmes, in which money is automatically deducted from our bank accounts and invested directly in the funds we select. This, too, compels us to make savings. To further boost our salvation, we might commit to rounding up our mortgage check to the nearest $100, converting the $1,423 mortgage payment to $1,500, therefore, accelerating the principal repayment on our loan. Because we have to pay the mortgage each month, this is an easy habit to develop. Your mortgage company may even permit you to set up automatic payments that include the additional sum, committing you to make these extra payments each month.

I have never used the terrible term "budgeting" in any of this. It is a concept frequently commended by financial gurus. Nonetheless, when I ask people if they budget, the response is nearly invariably "no" — and for a good reason. Budgeting is ineffective for the majority of people. When we budget, the goal is to examine our monthly expenses, identify savings and spending restraint areas, and then save whatever money remains at the end of the month.

The issue is that we frequently reach the end of the month with no money to save. Along the way, we succumbed to temptation, splurged, blew our budget, and ended the month feeling guilty about our frivolous spending. Budgeting, in general, is an unpleasant and stressful affair. We always spend more than we intend, which leaves us feeling guilty.

That is why, it is preferable to disregard the budget and instead begin saving money as soon as we receive our salary. This is the time-honored technique of "paying yourself first." We promptly deduct 10% or 15% of our salary and then push ourselves to exist on the remainder. We are sure that we have protected our savings. That means we may spend our leftover income anyway we choose, without worrying about some stupid budget or if there will be enough money left over to save. You are tempted to make a budget, are not you? Simply say no.

8.2 Why You Should Save?

Make saving money a routine. Take a cue from the classic film The Richest Man in Babylon and pay yourself first and foremost! Pay yourself a percentage of the money you have earned each time you receive a paycheck before doing anything else with the money you have made. Pay yourself first before you go on and pay the rest of the expenses!

You should also scrutinize your expenditures. Treat your life like a CEO would treat his firm, and eliminate anything or objects that show superfluous. David Bach is credited with inventing the infamous "Latte Effect." If you could resist purchasing a $4 cup of coffee every morning and instead put the money into savings, money would begin to accumulate slowly but steadily. In this case, the ancient saying "A penny saved is a penny earned" is exemplified to the highest degree.

There is a significant distinction between being thrifty and being inexpensive. A thrifty person is prudent with their finances. The motives of someone cheap are primarily selfish, with little interest in helping others.

Should we spend it or save it? Of course, this is necessary to maintain the money in circulation. Furthermore, what is the point of living if we do not make full use of it?

Just make sure you do not waste it all! Collection agencies will keep phoning you at all hours, making it impossible to enjoy life. Take it from me when I say that they can be pretty irritating.

Much of what we acquire is unnecessary and adds little or no value to our lives regarding material possessions. Such purchases are made on the spur of the moment (thus the term "impulse buy"), and corporations are well aware of the various techniques that may be used to persuade you to purchase their goods.

Refrain from giving in to these temptations. Some things are not required. You have already demonstrated that you are not reliant on whatever it is by making it thus far without it.

Yet another fantastic piece of straightforward advice that I received from the legendary Robert Kiyosaki, author of the Rich Dad, Poor Dad trilogy. Kiyosaki recommends depositing a tiny portion of your salary into three separate "Piggy Banks," one for each of your children. Use one piggy bank for savings, investment, and donating to a good cause (or tithing). Deposit the money in an equal amount for each of the three. Do not deceive yourself in this situation.

Make a tiny proportion of your income your default until it becomes a habit and does not send you into a state of financial shock. Once you begin putting aside a small amount of money at a time, you will experience a great sense of relief, knowing that you have some financial stability. Eventually, you will like watching your money increase, and you will go out of your way to begin depositing money into each bank account you have opened.

As your money accrues interest, start allowing it to generate income for you. When it comes to compounding interest, Einstein said it best: "Compounding interest is a mathematical phenomenon." "Amounts of compound interest are considered to be the eighth wonder of the universe. That which is understood is earned; that which is not understood is paid for."

Giving to charity is arguably one of the most essential and beneficial things that someone can do for themselves and their community. This unselfish gesture will not only benefit others, but it will also improve your personal qualities unconsciously, leading you to desire to earn more money to give more.

The key here is to be grateful for the money we do have. Our passion for money will become more robust due to our efforts to save and appreciate our hard-earned money. The money we save will serve as a magnet for more money.

We are going to go back to the beginning here; go out and purchase a piggy bank or a fishbowl, which is what I like. For this reason, I want to utilize something transparent to practically watch my money increase right in front of my eyes. You would have three different banks in an ideal world: saving for future expenses, investing, and donating to charity. You should aim to set away 10% of each paycheck as a savings account.

To get our feet wet, let's start with only one piggy bank for this month to gain our bearings. Deposit into this bank with all of your spare change and spare dollars, as well as the money you save from any small expenses you eliminate. Allow time to pass as you continue to deposit money into the account and avoid calculating it. I ACTUALLY MEAN IT! Set a date for counting that is several months away, but do not count every day. Allow it to continue to develop, and allow your mind to wonder how much is truly within.

Money is attracted to money. As your money continues to expand and grow, more money will be drawn to it, which will continue indefinitely. Subconsciously, you will begin to desire to save money on everything you purchase. Be patient and wait for the right moment. In a year, you will be overjoyed with your accomplishments.

Another strategy is to leave the store when you find something you "truly" desire and return later to avoid making an impulse buy. Be strong in this situation, resist the urge, and then consider whether or not you absolutely must have this thing. More often than not, you will discover that you can function very well without them.

Engage in only one type of business and be committed to it until you succeed or your experience indicates that you should quit it. Constant pounding on a single nail will usually eventually drive it home, allowing it to be clinched. When a man's full attention is focused on a single thing, his mind will continuously offer valuable enhancements that he would miss if a dozen distinct subjects engaged his brain at the same time. Considerable fortunes have gone through a man's fingers due to his involvement in too many jobs at the same time. The adage about not having too many irons in the fire at once makes logic.

8.3 The Moral Responsibility of Paying Forward

The act of giving to others who are less fortunate is a beautiful method to attract what you desire into your life. I understand that you may be thinking, "I don't have anything to contribute." The reality is that you do.

While reading this book, you may fall to the notion that you have nothing of worth. Allow yourself to let go of the idea of being nothing; you are more valuable than you think. It is essential to recognize the fact that you are on the path to attracting success.

Even if you do not have any actual, worldly items, such as money, you may still help someone in need by sending a simple prayer or sending love to them. This gesture is potent since it helps to boost up both the person in need and oneself at the same time.

"Helping others achieve what they want first," as the late great Zig Ziglar once said, "is the most effective method to acquire what you want." This is applicable in many aspects of life. Begin by being friendly and kind to others. Your inner self will release serotonin or 5-HTP, which will be contagious (a neurotransmitter involved with happiness). You will notice an immediate improvement in your disposition. Even a simple gesture, such as holding a door for someone, can have a significant impact, and you will notice it. It all adds up, and the more compassion you show others, the more kindness you will receive in return, and even more so. This can also be categorized as a violation of the law of Karma.

What goes around comes around twice as much, so why not give out what you would like to be given back in exchange? Prepare to be blessed with something much better than you imagined. You have absolutely nothing to lose and everything to gain by participating. Come from a position of kindness and compassion.

Although it may not appear that you are making a difference in the world with each tiny deed, in reality, you are. When you act kind, the person who is on the receiving end will experience an emotional uplift as a result. You will experience an even more significant emotional uplift as a result of this. More than that, everyone in the vicinity who witnesses this act of compassion will also experience a pleasant lift in their spirits. Although it may seem strange, those who are just seeing your act of kindness towards someone else will get a nice boost as well (a surge of serotonin). Love and compassion spread like wildfire.

The idea here is to act as though we already have more than we need. If you want to eat and live here, we encourage you to give whatever you have saved rather than purchasing an additional cup of coffee each day or another drink at the bar. If you pass a homeless person on your way to work every day, consider starting by placing some money in their cup to show your support.

What happens if you are scraping by and can't spare even a single cent? What are your options?

Do not be concerned; you can always say a prayer, send love (but not in public; we do not want to appear excessively strange), or act kindness for someone in need. Continue doing these activities as much as you can until they become ingrained in your personality. The benefits in exchange for your efforts will be substantial. This is a win-win situation!

Chapter 9: Money Management

Sensible money management is very straightforward: we must save consistently, limit risk, purchase a few funds, keep prices low, and keep a half-eye on taxes. As I hope, I have demonstrated in the past chapters, investing may be pretty straightforward.

And yet, it is far from simple. We commit various behavioural errors, including saving too little, being overconfident during periods of market growth, and losing faith during periods of market decline. That is not to say that we all make the same mental errors or exhibit the same behavioural idiosyncrasies. However, some of these anomalies are very widespread – and they adversely affect the investing performance of many people.

All of this reflect a partial rejection of traditional economics, which presupposes rational conduct. Rational? Consider that the next time you skip the gym, eat the chocolate you promised you would not touch, overspend at the mall, and build up another round of startling credit card bills.

9.1 Struggling to Save

Indeed, our behavioural difficulties begin with a lack of self-control, making it difficult to wait for gratification and result in far insufficient savings. This may have evolved as a result of natural selection. Our hunter-gatherer forefathers and mothers did not give much attention to retirement planning. Rather than that, they were concerned with survival, which meant consuming whatever and whenever possible. Perhaps it is unsurprising that deferring gratification is difficult for us today – and why we resort to every kind of deception to convince ourselves to save.

You could suppose that as an alternative for deception, we might try financial education. The issue is that schooling does not appear to be effective. We are all aware of the need for saving, but we consistently fall short. For instance, if we are asked whether we would be ready to forego some comforts to save an additional $100 per week a year from now, we could respond, "Yes." However, if we were asked if we would be willing to begin belt-tightening immediately, we would almost certainly decline. We know what is best for us in the long run, but it is all too simple to postpone because the future is so far. As in the sinner's prayer, "God, please save me — but not now."

While a lack of self-control is probably the primary reason we do not save enough, our profligacy may also be attributed to our insufficient math abilities. The majority of us do not carry financial calculators with us. Rather than that, when presented with common financial math issues, we make educated assumptions — and our estimates are frequently incorrect. For example, we may be aware of compounding, the process through which we make investment returns not just on our initial investment but also on prior years' earnings that we put back into our nest egg.

While we have a general understanding of how compounding works, we frequently underestimate its influence. This implies that we are unaware of the potential growth of our savings over time and so are not as driven to save as we should be. We grossly underestimate the cost of our loans. While we know that our credit cards carry a high-interest rate, we are unaware of the amount of interest we will accrue if we do not pay off our credit cards in full. Each month that we hold a balance on our credit card, we are charged interest on the outstanding sum. It is similar to investing, except that time is our adversary, not our ally.

9.2 Riding the Bull

If saving is a fight, investing is a war – and many of our wounds are inflicted on ourselves. Assume we are amid a stock market surge. At that point, our instinct is to be excessively cautious. As behavioural economists have shown, humans are naturally loss-averse, experiencing considerably more pain from losses than profits. Indeed, scholarly research indicates that the pain associated with losses is twice as significant as the joy related to wins.

During the stock market rebound stages, this loss aversion may drive us to avoid equities. Perhaps you've heard of the market's tremendous long-term gains. However, we are far more concerned with the prospect of catastrophic short-term losses. We despise the thought of investing a large sum of money in equities to watch the market crash. That would imply heinous losses — and agonising emotions of sorrow.

This helps explain the popularity of dollar-cost averaging and the practice of investing the same amount each month regardless of the market conditions. Dollar-cost averaging is hailed as a systematic, no-nonsense approach to stock investing. However, it is genuinely about investor psychology, assisting us in overcoming our aversion to investing and making the market fall more bearable. True, this month's investment may out to be a financial loss. However, we have the consolation of knowing that we will have another opportunity to purchase next month.

As the market continues to rise, our willingness to acquire equities increases somewhat. However, the scholarly study indicates that we will usually go toward the familiar when purchasing. Many people appear to suffer from home bias, which means that we prefer the stocks of our employer, local businesses, well-known blue-chip organisations, and enterprises whose goods we consume. When these equities are combined, they may produce an insufficiently diversified portfolio — yet this is the portfolio we are comfortable holding.

Meanwhile, we avoid exotic assets like commodities and foreign equities, even though these exotic investments may reduce our portfolio's overall volatility. However, when the rise gets momentum, such unusual assets may appear less hazardous, especially if they are recording significant returns. We are predisposed to seek patterns in the market's wild gyrations, eliciting all manner of confident projections. This pattern recognition leads us to extrapolate current returns and, before long, we conclude that the rising market will continue to rise. Forget about history's vast arc. We are far more impacted by recent weeks and months.

We will quickly forget about the market's uncertainties. Rather than that, we convinced ourselves that stocks were bound to rise. We may even conclude that we anticipated the rally. Due to this hindsight bias, the market appears more predictable, which encourages us to pursue our present investment hunches.

Additionally, the soaring market boosts our confidence, as we credit our investing profits to our genius and become obsessed with outperforming the market. This results in us placing larger financial wagers and purchasing actively managed funds. Men are more sensitive to all of this, with a propensity to trade more, hoard more stocks, and pursue riskier stock investing techniques.

We could even be victims of the house money effect. As with early-evening casino gamblers, our investing success may give us the impression that we are ahead of the game — and can afford to take additional risk. True, there may be warning indicators, such as excessive valuations and cynical analysts. However, we dismiss inconvenient facts and pay minimal heed to statistical data. Rather than that, we cling to the arguments, anecdotes, and other shards of evidence that strengthen our case.

We connect hard effort with success by taking our cues from the workplace. Additional research and trading appear to result in more remarkable results. Indeed, some of our stocks have increased in value, and we take tremendous joy in converting our paper earnings to actual cash. The issue is that selling winners result in investment expenses and significant tax liabilities if we trade in a taxable account.

Money, on the other hand, is only a portion of the payout. Put aside your concerns about accomplishing goals. Wall Street evolved as a source of entertainment. We enjoy the sensation of being in sync with the market's movement. We derive pleasure from purchasing and selling. Trading enables us to develop an emotional connection to our money and a sense of control. We developed an affinity for our investments. We were delighted to get 100 shares of a hot initial public offering. We enjoy the cachet associated with hedge fund ownership. We invest in socially responsible mutual funds and use our own to demonstrate our political commitment.

Trading aggressively and purchasing exotic assets early in the rise would have appeared dangerous. It now feels nearly secure, in part because so many people are doing the same thing. We gravitate toward popular assets for the affirmation we receive from others around us. Naturally, popularity is an excellent indicator when choosing a movie, a car, or a restaurant. However, crowds are perilous in the financial world. If an investment is prevalent, it is likely expensive. When everyone has purchased, there is no one left to buy. When will the next bear market begin? It is probably not all that far away.

9.3 Losing Our Nerve

Market rallies frequently persist far longer than doubters anticipate. Bearish investors say the end is near, only to have their projections shattered by rising share prices. However, as mother warned, "It would inevitably end in tears." When an investment becomes extremely popular, you can be reasonably make sure that difficult times are ahead — even if you cannot predict when those difficult times will occur.

When equities initially begin to fall, we dismiss it. However, as the fall continues, our confidence erodes. We are no longer confident in our forecasts and are less eager to trade. Rather than projecting infinite gains, we are now assuming the market will continue to decline. Fearful of additional losses, some panic and sell. However, many people freeze. We tend to regret commission errors more than omission errors. That we are losing money is terrible enough. However, if we attempt another transaction and it fails, we will feel much worse.

As we bite our nails and hold our breath, we are impacted by the endowment effect, the human propensity to go beyond market pricing and ascribe additional worth to the possessions we possess. This is why we hold on to the investments our parents left us. We feel that our portfolios have performed better than they have in reality and that our assets and residences are worth more than their current market value.

Similarly, when we psychologically evaluate our stocks and mutual funds, we may be anchored by the price we paid or the amount we could have gotten had we sold at the market's peak — and we are vehemently opposed to trading for less. Experts discuss risk aversion. However, we are loss averse. We despise the prospect of financial loss. Indeed, we will continue to hold a risky, poorly diversified portfolio in the hope of "getting even, then getting out." Selling entails abandoning all hope of recouping our losses and acknowledging our error. We may even "double down" on failing stock holdings, purchasing additional shares and incurring more significant risks to recoup our losses swiftly.

It is unlikely that our investments will be the source of our greatest misery. We anticipate stocks to behave unpredictably. Rather than that, we might get particularly uneasy if ostensibly secure investments prove to be hazardous. We are unconcerned with a 1% fall in the stock market. However, we are concerned about the possibility that our money market fund's $1 share price may "break the buck" and plummet to 99 cents.

Loss aversion is not always detrimental. It may protect us from selling at the worst possible time during a down market. If we have well-diversified portfolios, it is usually prudent for us to hold onto our investments. However, we would likely fare much better if we increased our stock purchases when prices fell rather than freezing. Market dips are a source of opportunity. Unfortunately, for many, they represent another opportunity to make other errors.

As is the case with our efforts to save, many of our financial mistakes may be linked to evolutionary psychology. Our forefathers and mothers survived because they worked hard, looked for patterns, imitated others, and feared loss. However, these characteristics might work against us in today's economic environment. Forget about blaming our parents for everything. The actual perpetrators, it appears, are our cave-dwelling forefathers.

9.4 Acquiring a Grip

What is the remedy for all of this? Hopefully, a little self-awareness can assist us in avoiding certain traps. If we bear in mind our numerous mental errors and attempt to remain focused on economic realities, perhaps we will act a bit more prudently and with a little more humility in the markets.

Nonetheless, just as we manipulated ourselves to increase our savings, we may need to influence ourselves into better investment behaviour. Standard financial theory instructs us to construct well-diversified portfolios and then focus on the portfolio's risk and return characteristics. However, many people struggle with this instead of obsessing over the success of each investment they hold. If you fall into this category, you may want to consider investments that combine various market sectors into a single portfolio.

Numerous 401 (k) plans are doing precisely that, realising that employees frequently struggle to invest wisely. They have expanded their plan's investment options by adding what is known as life cycle funds, target-date retirement funds, or lifestyle funds. These funds provide one-stop shopping for investors by pooling various market sectors into a single mutual fund. Within the fund, specific sectors may be soaring while others are collapsing. However, all shareholders perceive a single share price that is reasonably stable in its performance.

However, just adding such assets to a 401 (k) is insufficient. The issue is that many employees do not contribute to their 401 (k) plans and, if they do, make poor investment choices. To address this not-so-beneficial neglect, several employers are now automatically enrolling employees in their 401 (k) plans and designating these one-stop-shopping funds as the default investment choice for their goals. Employees can always opt-out of enrollment and often invest in other assets.

However, inertia is a powerful force—and many employees do not opt-out, resulting in their saving more and investing more prudently than they would otherwise.

If you often sabotage your investing performance, you might also consider hiring a financial adviser. Consider the adviser's job as a coach, someone who will push you to save consistently, diversify widely, stay the course during times of market volatility, and make more informed financial decisions in other aspects of your life. The adviser's role is to steer you away from self-inflicted investing wounds and toward more prudent financial conduct. Your adviser may not give you market-beating returns—but they may help you grab a more significant share of the market's recovery and avoid falling far below market averages.

Even with the assistance of an expert, you may struggle to cope with the market's insanity. However, your concerns may decrease with time. Our risk tolerance may fluctuate in lockstep with the markets. However, it does alter with experience. Younger investors are said to be more risk-tolerant, which is accurate in terms of time horizon. However, elder investors may have an edge when it comes to mental toughness since they have lived through several market cycles and are familiar with what to expect. A 25-year-old with 60% of his wealth in stocks may be scared when market prices fall — whereas a 65-year-old with the same portfolio may be entirely at ease. Are you feeling uneasy? Perhaps you should give it some time.

9.5 Losing with Elegance

As with family, our lifestyle choices may have a significant impact on our wealth. There is an apparent consequence: If we are excessive spenders, we will save less and require a larger nest egg to maintain the same standard of living in retirement. This may mean postponing retirement while we accumulate additional funds, and even then, we may have to reduce our quality of life once we retire.

We identify riches with its accoutrements, such as expensive clothing and fancy automobiles. However, these adornments are not indicative of riches. Rather than that, they symbolise money spent — and the individuals involved are the poorer as a result. Indeed, the neighbourhood's wealthiest family may reside in the tiniest house with the oldest automobile. Their thrifty nature enables them to save profusely. This is not desired. Spendthrifts and misers alike do not merit our praise. Instead we should aim to find the proper balance, spending money on the things that matter most to us while still saving enough to accomplish our goals.

Our lifestyle choices are not just financial. Additionally, there are health concerns. If we smoke two packs a day, consume large amounts of alcohol, and do not exercise, we risk deteriorating our health, limiting our capacity to work, and incurring enormous medical costs. We are also likely to reduce our life expectancy, which means we may not need to fund such a lengthy retirement. However, I imagine that it will be of little consolation.

9.6 Playing The odds

Even if we exercise caution, we may find ourselves on the losing end of the genetic lottery and face physical issues. Alternatively, our spouse or one of our children may get unwell. Once again, this may impair our capacity to work and result in significant medical and other expenses. This takes us to the third component, luck, which affects our health and professions.

We want to believe that if we work hard enough, we will advance in our careers. However, life does not always work that way. Perhaps our adopted job is in a failing industry, and our efforts to save are thwarted by regular periods of unemployment. Similarly, maybe we possess a set of abilities that are in short supply. We frequently hear about hedge fund managers amassing millions, if not billions, of dollars. These individuals possess skills that are highly appreciated in today's market. However, someone with the same combination of abilities living in a different era or place may not be regarded nearly as highly—and may be considered modest members of the middle class.

What is the moral of this story? There are certain circumstances over which we have little or no influence, such as whether our job experiences financial difficulties or our parents are affluent or impoverished. However, there are certain variables that we can influence, like our spending habits, our health, and our efforts to raise money-savvy children. It is similar to investing. We do not affect how the markets behave. However, we influence how much money we save, how much risk we accept, and how much money we spend on investing fees.

The message is that we should refrain from feeling awful about the things we cannot control—instead concentrate on the ones we can. We may never achieve a six-figure salary or have a portfolio worth seven figures. However, we can retain that sense of control over our financial lives and extract an abundance of enjoyment from the cash we have.

Chapter 10: A Sophisticated Analysis of the Concept of Money

When it comes to dispelling our most irrational money beliefs, the sense of ownership must be emphasized. Yes, because the concept of possession is erroneous when it comes to the people like children, partners, friends, etc. and the goods and properties we own at any particular time in our lives. Possession is a subset of control, and control, as I have explained numerous times, is an illusion. We frequently lose control of ourselves, our emotions, and our surroundings. Would not it be wonderful if we could? Willpower and a desire for power are two separate concepts. We put ourselves to the test by taming our will, and we learn to accept the tangible limitations of our efforts. When it comes to making a difference and accomplishing a goal, words are equally important. Here is a chance I would like to offer for describing our relationship with money, regardless of our financial condition. We are money's custodians, not its owners.

Money can never genuinely be claimed as one's own. Choosing to be a carrier of money rather than an owner is another deliberate step toward understanding the nature of reality. It is not only an issue of spiritual interpretation; it is a fact that defies a superficial and worldly viewpoint. Money is given to us only to the extent that we can manage it. True, our essence, ethical principles, and life priorities we assign to ourselves do not change. Above all, the sense of being here, of being present, has been with us since the moment we have become aware of our existence. This sentiment has not changed and will never change. It has never been a child and will never be an adult.

Perceiving ourselves as stewards of our material assets rather than owners is crucial because it impacts our relationship with money. We are more at ease now that we have let go of the sense of "having something to lose." When you live with this emotion, your financial condition improves noticeably. While this may appear to be a paradox, we believe that we may finally accept prosperity in this mindset. Stress reduction increases our attentiveness and effectiveness by removing unreasonable emotional fears from our thinking. The desire for control, on the other hand, exacerbates the problem. Relationships and business interactions deteriorate. It may proceed to psychosis if it becomes a thorn in the person's side. This way of thinking, which is considered normal in the capitalist culture in which we live, leads to fury and frustration.

Along with envy, there is resentment toward the world's vast wealth being concentrated in the hands of a few families of big bankers. At the same time, the vast mass of humanity lives in poverty or complete misery. I am the first to admit the presence of this
self-proclaimed elite, but the same ownership laws apply to them as well despite appearances, and they are not entitled to interfere with the money intended for me. Unless we give them this power, truly wealthy and influential people can manage a more considerable sum of money simply because it is required for the earthly task at hand. The amount of money we can have is determined by our attitude toward life and our

particular life mission. Being wealthy, or feeling wealthy, is a state of mind that is unrelated to a bank account. I met rich people who acted impoverished, counting their pennies to save them. For what purpose? Because they were hungry and were afraid of losing their position. Then I came across people who appeared impoverished but cheerfully shared what they had. I saw disadvantaged people who were happier than many wealthy people.

Existence is designed in such a way that we are rewarded for benefiting one another. This means that the money we get is proportional to the benefit someone can get from what we do. This is also true for drug dealers, exploiters, and thieves. Because, even in these cases, it is a matter of providing a service with the potential to earn a large amount of revenue. The purpose in these cases is not to give an exceptional service but to exploit people's vulnerabilities and foster their addictions.

If the result of our activities is unethical, if we cause suffering while benefiting ourselves, karma will take over. We will be called upon to settle the bill sooner or later. If the energy we generate is malignant, self-righteous, or authoritarian, the cosmos will return it to us. Money is not the source of the problem. Remember that money is always a neutral means of exchange. What comes back to us is the result of our deeds, hearts, and honesty, combined with excellent mental planning.

There are no accessible routes to true riches, and there is no way to avoid danger to retain our assumed daily assurance.

Only our dreams exist, as does our inclination to pamper and care for them the same way we do for those we love. Who knows, maybe the imprint we leave on this planet may help it improve? It is up to us to decide how to spend our lives, and we must accept responsibility for our decisions. This is the fundamental nature of free will. In either scenario, addressing someone's requirements is an essential part of financial success. Those that benefit a considerable number of others are rewarded in life. It is only natural to become one of the world's wealthiest people if you reach the stage of delivering helpful services to billions of people, like Amazon, Facebook, and Microsoft did.

10.1 A Connecting Element Between the Body, Mind, Emotions, and Money

Have you ever noticed how frequently people who have a poor connection with money and are focused on it, including those who have a lot of it, do not appear attractive? In other words, they do not seem to be in good health. This is since health and money are intimately intertwined. The tranquillity that arises from a mind that works in harmony with his goals leads to more stable emotions and a tension-free physical body. Avoiding the concern that comes from believing that the money we make is never enough or from the mistake of saving at all costs to keep our money. As a result, we may say that money influences health.

Let us now move on to another topic: Reality Transurfing and the advanced quantum research conducted by very open-minded doctors such as Joe Dispenza and Roy Martina.

Reality Transurfing is a method that offers a complete alignment with the existence between the progression of our lives and the Law of Attraction. Doctor Dispenza has created something similar. He is a fine connoisseur of quantum physics applied to the interactions between our daily life and what we desire. A way to enhance the ability to determine the future we want, the projects we most care about. He is also well-versed in using verbal intentions to enhance bodily healing from illnesses and accidents. This happens not by a magical effect. It is not a spell, but because both the metabolism and the immune system undergo a psychosomatic influence. If we know how to reduce stress best, we can avoid hindering the self-regenerative processes of our body.

Roy Martina and his wife Joy hold Quantum Healing courses characterized by meditations and psychoactive practices that maintain the cognitive purpose of the connection between the surrounding environment and our inner well-being. There would also be Theta Healing to talk about, another valid system of improvements in health, love, and wealth, but this is not the appropriate place. While avoiding digressions, I would like to emphasize the importance of taking a holistic approach to consider the interconnectedness of our actions and their consequences, both on ourselves and in the fields, we work regardless of whether our goal is a better working profession, more satisfying interpersonal relationships, or the improvement of our financial condition,

The criteria I mentioned here above are the result of rigorous interdisciplinary studies and have proven to work. This is because they involve all three of our bodies: mental, physical, and emotional. They increase the possibility of activating the Law of Attraction for the object of our desire. (All of which I have explained in-depth in one of my books named "Unconditional Love"). Imagining future prosperity as though it were nowhere is an essential mental exercise. However, completing this vision right necessitates emotional participation, experiencing the joy of accomplishment, and perceiving as many specifics about the future as possible. We already feel a sense of connection. In this manner, we bring something that does not yet exist in the current era but artistically corresponds to one of the multiverse's possibilities. The more we determine what is perfect for us, the more we know ourselves and the outside world, the more it could come true. The purpose of Reality Transurfing and its author, Vadim Zeland, is to allow us to actively choose the path we want to take for the rest of our lives and to make this notion very obvious in our minds, and therefore very powerful. The rest is up to the universe to decide whether or not to provide it to us.

Throughout these visualization tasks, we are writing our wishes on parchment in a romantic metaphor. Then, like a message in a bottle, it is wrapped up and sent out into the sea. The important thing is that we take care of our part and aim our will toward the vision we want to realize. It makes no difference what the sea of existence thinks of what we have spoken, but it does make a difference in our state of mind to know that we have done everything possible. As a result, we have nothing to regret or feel guilty about, spiritually and practically; knowing that we have done our best gives us a tremendous sense of inner peace.

In this passage, I hope I have tickled the curiosity of those readers who still do not know these developments in personal growth and who can deepen the topic, thanks to the mighty internet search tool.

10.2 Attracting Financial Prosperity and the Power Concept

In this specific section, we will look at the concept of power, how to win the jackpot, and how to attract financial wealth through musical frequencies. Knowing how to filter out irrelevant information to resolve a particular circumstance allows us to avoid one of the Internet's disadvantages: cognitive overload. In this book, I hope to give a reason for utilizing the fantastic tool that is the Internet.

Word knowledge is essential in this setting because we begin to define our environment through words. So, what exactly does the phrase "power" mean? The ability to act on something or exert influence in the manner desired. The control concept we have experienced is an illusion when examined from a broader reality lens, always looking out for the unexpected. "Grant me the serenity to accept what I cannot change, the courage to change what I can, and the insight to know the difference," says the Serenity Prayer.

In general, it is preferable to gain small percentages on a daily, weekly, or monthly basis rather than risking a larger sum by leveraging power, such as by lingering in the trade area. At the very least, if we are talking about large numbers, it should be in the $2-3,000 range. Regardless of our subjective ideas of what constitutes a lot and what constitutes a little, we talk about the money we have. It can make sense to bet on a multiplier effect that is sufficiently secured against deposit loss with a few hundred dollars. Furthermore, to cover the costs of specialized operations, closures, openings, and fees. This is a gambling reference.

With this concept, we are getting closer to actual betting, where risk and chance play a larger part and the variables we can control grow less. Moving on to systems for increasing your chances of success in card games like poker, roulette strategies, and slot machine tips. These can be enchanting because there is a lot of psychology and mentalism involved. We are now entering a more preoccupied realm with faith, fate, and predestination than religion. Lottery ticket customers can be divided into four types.

On the one hand, some are greedy gamblers. They are obsessed with winning, as does anyone addicted to the gambling devil, with all it involves, like progressive impoverishment and degradation of social relations. Then some gamble in the hope of resolving a vexing economic dilemma. They are typically afraid and unable to consider alternatives.

The anxiety levels in the following two categories are lower. In their effort to avoid the core cause of concern, control mania, they are frequently non-existent. More quiet people are more secure and aware of how they handle their personal and economic resources.

Some play on an irregular basis and with little hope of winning, a once-in-a-while indugence during a coffee break. Finally, some people have a significant idea but are unable to fund it in any way. As a result, unexpected help may appear to support them in their day-to-day responsibilities. These categories of winners have one thing in common: they are all working to improve their money management skills because it is difficult to manage changes in one's life, social relationships, or finances when a large sum of money arrives unexpectedly. Many people fail this exam far more often than they realize. Friends and family members are perceived to be driven by a desire to win money, regardless of whether they are or are not.

Our perceptions that nothing that happens to us is permanent help us in a variety of ways. To begin with, it soothes us because those who understand how to develop a material advantage recognize that even if they lose it, they can rebuild it. As long as there is life, there is hope. Then, because we are fighting common sense while clinging to what we have, are we confident that our attachment to a property and a specific sum of money would benefit us and fulfil our desires? A person's professional life can become so
engaging that he loses sight of his personal life, friends, and family.

It is feasible that a severe financial loss will correct this imbalance, leading the activity in progress to fail and the employee to seek employment elsewhere. In response, there will be extreme rage, despair, and a sense of injustice at first. However, when something that allows him to live a better life becomes available, such as a lighter job with more free time, that person would recognize that a terrible incident was simply a shift he did not want to make. A decision was not made; instead, it was postponed due to some habit and fear. As a result, a given incident can be regarded from two perspectives: one that is more casual and superficial, and one that is more complete, taking into account all of the positives and bad that occurred. Life can be compared to a chessboard at times. There are those who look at it from a balanced perspective, focusing on the positions of all the chess pieces, and those who try to build an entire picture from a higher vantage point.

Finally, I would like to spend a few words examining the sound frequencies that appear to attract money and good fortune. My recommendation is to listen to them since it will help you keep your financial focus. Music is pure vibration; it constantly acts and interacts with the subconscious even while engaged in another activity, such as cooking, housekeeping, gardening, or reading this book. There are beneficial frequencies, such as the well-known 432 Hz, which is also employed in a large number of albums. Music is widely recognized as a sort of therapy, capable of soothing the mind and creating altered states of consciousness. This is not to say that these songs are utterly effective at increasing our wealth. Nothing is guaranteed except death and taxes. Each of us is unique, with our own particular experience and relationship with money. These noises can be used as a supplement and should be regarded as such. It is simply available via the Internet, and it is free to try. Different frequencies used to attract money energy and facilitate its entry into our lives are 417, 528, and 639 Hz. Theta waves and binaural beats are an intriguing kind and are great for keeping us company as we sleep because of their calming nature.

10.3 Work on Your Intellect

Nobody is a born financial genius. Every wealthy person has figured out how to win in the money game, and you can too. Keep in mind that your mantra is, "If they can do it, so can I!"

Becoming wealthy is not so much about financial gain as it is about the person you must become in character and intellect in order to achieve wealth. I would want to share with you a little-known secret: the quickest method to become and remain wealthy is to work on growing yourself! The objective is to develop into a "successful" person. Again, the external world is only a reflection of the internal reality. You are the root; the fruits are your actions.

There is a proverb that I like: "You take yourself wherever you go." If you develop yourself into a successful person, both in terms of character and mind, you will naturally succeed in everything you do. You will get the ability to make unrestricted choices. You will develop the inner strength and ability to choose any employment, business, or investment field with confidence. This is the essence of this book. When you are a level 5 individual, you will receive level 5 outcomes. However, if you can develop into a level 10 individual, you will receive level 10 results.

But heed this caution. If you do not perform the inner work and somehow make a lot of money, it will almost certainly be a stroke of luck, and you will almost certainly lose it. However, if you develop into a successful "person" on the inside and out, you will not only achieve success, but you will also maintain it, grow it, and most importantly, you will be truly happy.

The wealthy recognize that the order of success is BE, DO, and HAVE.
Poor and middle-class people feel that having, doing, and being is the order of success.

The poor and the majority of middle-class people feel that "if I had a lot of money, I could accomplish whatever I wanted and be successful."

Rich people understand, "If I achieve success, I will be able to do whatever it takes to obtain what I desire, including a large sum of money."

Another secret that only the wealthy understand: the purpose of wealth creation is not to amass large sums of money; the purpose of wealth creation is to assist you in developing into the best person you can possibly be. Indeed, it is the purpose of all goals: to develop as a person. Madonna, the world-renowned singer and actress, was questioned about why she changed her character, music, and style every year. She stated that music was her vehicle for expressing her "self" and that reinventing herself each year forced her to mature into the person she desired.

In a nutshell, success is defined by "who" rather than "what." The good news is that your "person" is completely trainable and learnable. I should be aware. While I am far from flawless, when I compare who I am today to who I was twenty years ago, I see a definite line between "me and my wealth" then and "me and my wealth" now. I discovered my path to success, and you can as well. That is why I am in the business of training. Personally, I know that practically everyone can be coached to succeed. I was taught to succeed, and now I am able to teach tens of thousands of others. Training is effective!

Another significant distinction I have discovered between the wealthy and the poor and middle classes is that the wealthy are specialists in their fields. The middle class is mediocre in their field, and the impoverished are mediocre in their field.

How proficient are you in your field? How competent are you in your field? Do you desire an entirely unbiased method of knowing? Consider your paycheck. That will provide you with all of the information you require. It is straightforward: to earn the best compensation, you must be the best.

Jim Rohn's adage, "If you continue to do what you have always done, you will continue to receive what you have always gotten," makes perfect sense here.

You are already familiar with "your" approach; what you need to learn are some fresh ones. That was the impetus for me to write this book. My objective is to provide you with some new mental files to supplement the ones you already possess. New files imply new modes of thought, new acts, and thus new outcomes.

That is why it is critical for you to continue learning and growing.

According to physicists, nothing in this universe is static. Everything alive is in perpetual flux. Consider any plant. If a plant does not grow, it dies. It is the same for humans and all other living organisms: if you do not grow, you will perish.

One of my favorite quotes comes from novelist and philosopher Eric Hoffer, who stated, "The learners will inherit the earth, while the learned will be magnificently equipped to survive in a world that no longer exists." Another way of putting it is that if you do not continue to study, you will fall behind.

Poor people assert that they cannot afford money owing to a lack of time or funds. On the other hand, wealthy individuals identify with Benjamin Franklin's quote: "If you believe education is costly, try ignorance." You have probably heard this before: "knowledge is power," and "power" refers to the capacity to act.

The only method I know for you to have the money you desire is to master the money game from beginning to end. You must develop the skills and tactics necessary to increase your income, manage your money properly, and invest it successfully. Insanity is defined as repeatedly doing the same thing and expecting different results. Consider that if what you have been doing was effective, you would already be wealthy and content. Anything else that comes to mind as a reaction is merely an excuse or justification.

I am sorry for being so direct about it, but that is, in my opinion, my job. I feel that a competent educator will always demand more of you than you are willing to give. Otherwise, why on earth would you require one? As a counsellor, my objective is to train you, inspire you, motivate you, coax you, and help you see what is holding you back in vivid detail. In a nutshell, to do everything it takes to propel you forward in life. If necessary, I will go to any length to make you 10 times happier and a hundred times wealthier. If you are seeking for Pollyanna, you have come to the wrong place. Let's proceed if you wish to relocate quickly and permanently.

Success is a skill that can be acquired. You can acquire the ability to succeed at anything. If you want to improve your golf game, you can. If you want to learn how to play the piano well, you can. If you sincerely desire happiness, you can learn how to achieve it. If you want to become wealthy, you can learn how. It makes no difference where you are at the moment. It makes no difference where you begin. What matters is your readiness to learn.

This is also true as you develop in the mentality department — many things that previously loomed hugely no longer does. Consider anything that was once an all-consuming, monstrous fear that you overcame and is now a pipsqueak of a memory if you can recall it at all: your first day at a new job, having your first child, or asking a friend for help. At the time, the discomfort was so great that you feared you would explode, but today, when you reflect on these worries, they feel quite unnecessary.

As you evolve, it is beneficial to remember that all the seemingly impossible roadblocks and fears you are currently encountering on your path to success will eventually become little pieces falling through the cracks of your memory. Consider looking back on them in the future while enjoying your success. In the future, you will know for certain that these unhelpful ideas and beliefs are not true, that you possess the powerful mentality necessary to disable them, and that those false beliefs were always bad for your mental health.

I recall back in the day when I was actively working on my shaky relationship with money, having a hard time believing all the hoopla about mentality. All the screaming and raving about positive thinking, faith, appreciation, and awareness — seriously, there had to be more to becoming wealthy than that. I anticipated that the process of reorganizing one's financial position would be more Rubik's Cube-like or at the very least the arduous equivalent of attending graduate school or ascending a mountain with a huge, clinging child on one's back. But to discover that an unshakeable commitment to wealth — a commitment, of all things! — was the primary distinction between my wounded heart and all those folks living large and in charge? What do you think I am, a loser?

Nature makes it simple; humans make it difficult.

Of course, getting rich entails relentless, scary, and dramatic jumps into the unknown, but the real transformation occurs between your ears. And I want to emphasize that it is not difficult. I can virtually promise that you have worked harder at other things in your life than you will need to work to become a financial winner. I am not saying that you will not have to work hard, but my life with money is a lot easier than my life without it ever was.

It is similar to how when you get in shape following a major spell of lethargic slobbiness, you begin eating better, walk taller, and become more focused, happy, confident, energetic, flirtatious, and well-shaven. If you want to alter your life, alter your life. And here's the wonderful additional prize for controlling your attitude, as if becoming wealthy is not awesome enough: Once you begin altering your thinking and entering the flow with money, your energy and many other aspects of your life will begin to transform as well. When you alter your financial reality, it is not just about watching your bank balance rise; it is about who you have to become in order for that growth to occur. You have to let go of your old ways of functioning and develop into someone who thinks big, someone who finds possibility more interesting than your excuses, someone who disregards your empty wallet, flimsy résumé, and lack of idea where you are going. If you can get wealthy, you can do anything, because not only are you the type of person who now makes money with every strategy he plays. The limiting beliefs that have kept you from making money are largely the same as those that keep you from losing twenty pounds, inspire you to date people who do not like you, and keep you clouded by doubt and indecision — the dam has been breached.

Conclusion

How have we progressed in our understanding of money? As with anything significant in our lives, it requires commitment, respect, and attention aimed at properly valuing it. Concentrating on money does not imply living for it or becoming obsessed with it. Obsessive behavior is never beneficial. When asked to discuss money, Arnold Schwarzenegger's speech about his six success rules and the importance of having a vision immediately comes to mind. Consider how thinking about that vision assists us in achieving it. The majority of people have no idea what they are doing or why they are doing it. They exist mechanically, without a sense of purpose. Money is merely a means of survival for these people, not a means of achieving something great.

The money is over there, awaiting our interpretation. However, this will never happen unless and until we give meaning to ourselves and our presence on Earth right now! Then you will notice that money will never be a problem in your life. It will flow like river water, as Heraclitus stated, because money is energy and must be allowed to flow as such. It comes, stays for the duration necessary, and then continues its journey. Withholding it for greed or fear, or squandering it, are the two most frequently adopted behaviors, both of which are disastrous because they disregard the energetic nature of the most powerful material realization tool we have. We are not here to be impoverished, nor are we here to be meaningless wealthy. We have come to this Earth to become wealthy, with all that this earthly existence has to offer, including money.

The strength of a vision also enables us to avoid self-doubt. Because doubt is such a powerful engine of intelligence and humility, it can act as a brake on us if we are afraid of falling short of... what? If we are here, how can we not be up to something? We have been placed here by something vast and mysterious, like gems on a necklace. With our horizontal gaze, we miss the drawing that is visible from above, believing that our position on the world's necklace is random. However, this is not the case; this is merely our impression, based on our limited perspective.

Fear of not achieving a goal is analogous to fear of the inevitability of death: what purpose does this fear serve? What have we got to lose? This is not to say that you should be reckless and dive headfirst into any case. As it is always the case, the optimal balance between inaction and haste lies somewhere in the middle. It is called discernment, and it is critical thinking's younger brother. It does not provide an emotional response to the stomach. It is the greatest gift that intelligence can bestow upon us. Thought without action is as ineffective as action without thought, and indeed, our inner equilibrium is determined by the relationship between right thought and right action (as it is well said in the Noble Eightfold Path).

Everything starts with your ideas. Train your thoughts and feelings, and your mind will soon be reprogrammed. You will begin to believe that you are deserving of everything. It must begin with your imagination, for it is only through your imagination that your desires will be realized.

Once you sincerely think that you deserve nothing less than the greatest and realize that it is within your grasp, you will arrive. You will obtain whatever you desire. As soon as possible, begin catching all negative ideas and replacing them with positive affirmations. Each individual has between 12,000 and 50,000 ideas each day (a wide range); the more introspective the thinker, the more thoughts. Now consider how many of those thoughts were pleasant and how many were negative. If you are dissatisfied with your current situation, I am guessing, I can deduce the majority of your thoughts. Begin by catching those self-defeating ideas! Eliminate them in the same manner as you would junk mail. Motivate your mind to think positively and guide that LEVER in the appropriate way. Once you begin to have a majority of good thoughts, you will reap favorable consequences. It is straightforward and uncomplicated. This will require some initial effort on your part, but over a short period of time, positive thinking will become second nature. It is critical that you do not allow anything or anyone to deter you from improving. Continue to grow, learn, and improve as a person. The universe has no bounds; the only ones you impose on it are those you impose on yourself. Proceed with caution. If wealth is what you seek, you can obtain it!!!This is real! You must continually strive to be one with money.

Consistency and integrity enable us to be as powerful and precise as an arrow shot from a firmly grasped bow. It is not simply a matter of ethics; it has become a way of life to achieve a balance of mind, body, and spirit. This approach encompasses a variety of topics, including money, interpersonal relationships, work, entertainment, and the issues we face in our lives.

For far too many people, money management is relegated to a Saturday hour spent balancing their chequebook, paying bills, and reviewing their mutual fund accounts. However, by compartmentalizing our finances in this way, we miss out on the opportunity to obtain so much more from our money. As you have probably concluded from the preceding pages, money is intricately linked to the rest of our life.

Each action we make — whether to purchase a new coat, go to the gym, or marry — has a financial consequence.

This is not to say that we should wait before making every financial action to consider the implications for our financial future. However, it does mean that we should ensure that our money and the rest of our life are in sync, which requires us to think much more carefully about how we spend our time and money. Consider the following seven instances.

- If our goal is to spend more time with our family, perhaps we should forego the high-spending lifestyle and opt for a smaller house closer to work, where we would not have to worry as much about the next pay raise and would not have to commute as far.

- If we truly want to quit our jobs and pursue something more meaningful but less lucrative, we should probably stop looking for salvation at the mall and start saving like crazy.

- If our jobs are insecure, we may want to avoid taking on a large mortgage and investing entirely in equities.

- If we are concerned that our family would be unable to function without us, it may be time to create a will, purchase life insurance, and verify that the correct beneficiaries are listed on our retirement funds.

- If we are actively preparing for a 30-year retirement, we may want to spend some time caring for our health, so that our bodies endure almost as long as our wits.

- If the last bear market left us with ulcers and sleepless nights, we may wish to resist the temptation to invest extensively in stocks during the following bull market.

- If we have frightening credit card bills and have no idea where the money went, it may be time to reconsider our spending habits—and how we spend it.

The bottom line is that we should work to ensure that money enriches rather than detracts from our lives. This is not an easy task. Market volatility can cause us to make rash decisions. Impulsive purchases have the potential to ruin our saving efforts. Concerns about our status can lead us to purchase an excessively large home and an excessively expensive car. However, while emotions can lead us wrong, a dose of common sense can help us stay on track. Let's face it; we all understand that we cannot spend our way to wealth. We have nagging worries that the large house, with its colossal mortgage and high utility bills, would generate a fortune for us. We understand that possessing a nice car does not automatically qualify us as wealthy. We have a strange hunch that the investment, which appears to be too good to be true, is in fact fraudulent.

After the financial crisis of 2008 and 2009, it is time to abandon wishful thinking and ostensibly miraculous remedies in favor of a few plain truths. No, we will not become wealthy overnight. However, if we are prudent with our money management, we may accumulate wealth over time — and, perhaps more importantly, we can get financial peace of mind along the way.

I would want to conclude by reminding you that you not only possess all you need to become wealthy right now, but also that the Universe is rooting for you and cheering you on, just as it does for every other living creature in nature. It is similar to when you see a friend who is so awesome, gorgeous, and talented and she sits about fretting about not knowing what she is doing, doubting her brilliance, and complaining about her weak chin—you want to shake her, wake her up, and create a PowerPoint presentation for her. You are so eager to demonstrate her grandeur and lovability that you really want her to grasp the fact that she is capable of accomplishing everything she sets her mind to. You want her to recognize the same qualities in herself that you do. This is how the Universe feels about you and your financial struggles. The Universe is having a heart attack over how great you are, and it is prepared to assist you in becoming wealthy. It is only waiting for you to get out of your own way, to stop focusing on your self-limiting beliefs, and to board the money party train.

Even when we attempt to establish a pension fund or a provision plan for our old age, we witness the energetic concept of money in action. Regardless of the fact that life occurs now, in the present, rather than 30-40 years from now (when we may already be dead), we can observe how ineffective personal economic management is in comparison to a profit-generating investment. The interest we earn on any type of active usage of money helps to maintain the intrinsic worth of our savings, so compensating for the increasing value loss of a particular sum of money.

Regardless of whether it is a speculative approach, listed shares, or something quieter and more stable, what moves money (given the relative risks) and does not erode our future purchasing power in the transactions in which we will invest it? Unless we are earning a sufficient money from a well-compensated job, it makes no sense that we are the only ones working, adding a modest percentage month after month to compensate for money's growing devaluation. While this may seem redundant, I want to emphasize how critical it is to put our money to work for us. Simple effort alone will not produce a result if we do not know, if we do not understand where we are going, starting with a basic understanding of ourselves.

In this regard, it is critical to advance our understanding. The desire to be more virtuous is an internal desire, and I hope that this book can activate and support it in some little way. Always keep in mind that those who do nothing, do not make mistakes and so cannot benefit from their experiences. I wish everyone of my readers' prosperity and happiness, so that you can find what you are looking for or, alternatively, position yourself to be found by the solutions the Universe has in store for you.

We inhabit an abundant universe in which you may obtain whatever amount of money you wish. When you genuinely intend to become wealthy, you open yourself up to the methods to accomplish that goal. Consider how incredible it will feel when you finally put an end to this financial beast. Think about the comfort and sense of achievement that comes from knowing that you and money are BFFs, coming and going in each other's life, cheerfully supporting one another, and braiding one another's hair. You have already accomplished the seemingly impossible — you have obtained the job for which you were "unqualified," gotten the lady or the man, relocated across the country, bought a house, and gotten the keys to your car out without shattering a window. You, too, are capable of wealth. You are unfathomably powerful and wonderful. Your destiny is to pursue your desires. You are destined to grow into the fullest manifestation of your one-of-a-kind and fantastic success story. You are destined for greatness.

I would like to wrap up with a devotion:

May this book serve as an encouragement to anyone who is hesitant to join the world's largest poker table. Whereas betting on ourselves gives meaning to the match, in the most serious game that exists, and which, precisely for this reason, should also be capable of irony: our lives.

www.ingramcontent.com/pod-product-compliance
Lightning Source LLC
Chambersburg PA
CBHW071355120626
46546CB00002B/707